The Healing Power of
Empathy

The Healing Power of

Empathy

*True Stories About
Transforming Relationships*

Edited by **Mary Goyer**

PuddleDancer
P R E S S

2240 Encinitas Blvd., Ste. D-911, Encinitas, CA 92024
email@PuddleDancer.com • www.PuddleDancer.com

For additional information:
Center for Nonviolent Communication
9301 Indian School Rd., NE, Suite 204, Albuquerque, NM 87112
Ph: 505-244-4041 • Fax: 505-247-0414 • Email: cnvc@cnvc.org • Website: www.cnvc.org

The Healing Power of Empathy
True Stories About Transforming Relationships
© 2019 PuddleDancer Press
A PuddleDancer Press Book

PuddleDancer Press, Permissions Dept.
2240 Encinitas Blvd., Ste. D-911, Encinitas, CA 92024
Tel: 1-760-652-5754 Fax: 1-760-274-6400
www.NonviolentCommunication.com Email@PuddleDancer.com

Ordering Information
Please contact Independent Publishers Group, Tel: 312-337-0747; Fax: 312-337-5985; Email: frontdesk@ipgbook.com or visit www.IPGbook.com for other contact information and details about ordering online.

Editor: Mary Goyer
Copyeditor: Tandem Editing LLC
Cover and interior design: Shannon Bodie, Lightbourne.com

Manufactured in the United States of America
1st Printing, June 2019
23 22 21 20 19   1 2 3 4 5
ISBN: 978-1-934336-17-5

Library of Congress Cataloging-in-Publication Data

Names: Goyer, Mary, editor.
Title: The healing power of empathy : true stories about transforming
  relationships / edited by Mary Goyer.
Description: Encinitas, CA : PuddleDancer Press, [2019]
Identifiers: LCCN 2018035907| ISBN 9781934336175 (trade paper : alk. paper) |
  ISBN 9781934336298 (ebook pdf) | ISBN 9781934336359 (mobi/kindle)
Subjects: LCSH: Empathy. | Interpersonal relations.
Classification: LCC BF575.E55 H43 2019 | DDC 155.4/1241--dc23
LC record available at https://lccn.loc.gov/2018035907

Endorsements of *The Healing Power of Empathy*

"You don't understand anything until you learn it more than one way' noted the late artificial intelligence researcher, Marvin Minsky. Nonviolent Communication (NVC) is often taught as a process for connecting with others, by following a sequence of steps. However, it can be challenging—and frustrating—to adapt this one method to the variety of situations we face. This book collects many stories of individuals skillfully applying NVC, with each told in the contributor's unique voice. I know of no single resource better than this book for those wanting to enrich their understanding of empathy."

> —EARL J. WAGNER, Compassionate Communication Trainer and
> Artificial Intelligence Software Engineer at Google

"This is the book I want everyone to read so they understand in a deeper way what empathy is, how it's transmitted, and what a healing impact it has on both giver and receiver. I keep it by my bedside and like to read one or two stories before I go to sleep to warm my heart and remind me of the kindness in the world. These real-life examples of the power of empathy serve to teach, model, and inspire in a transformative way no other book I know does. As I read the stories, it was like the empathy got absorbed into all the cells of my body, like an immersion into an empathy bath. I plan to add it to my resource list for workshops on NVC and empathy."

> —ALI MILLER, MFT, NVC-Based Therapist
> and Communication Coach

"If you ever wondered how people who are deeply committed to Nonviolent Communication live their path in their workplaces, families, and intimate relationships, this is the book for you. It permits the reader to take a peek into the daily lives and struggles of people who have been learning this work for decades, changing their language and their hearts along the way. It also reveals the odd and beautiful quiet that comes from seeing the world through a new lens. Read this book for inspiration, and then read it again for companionship."

> —SARAH PEYTON, author, *Your Resonant Self: Guided Meditations
> and Exercises to Engage Your Brain's Capacity for Healing*

"Inspiring and authentic! Real stories from real people sharing their transformative experiences of empathy in its many and glorious forms. Mary is the perfect person to have collected these stories. I hope you get the opportunity to be in the presence of her empathy."

—JEAN MORRISON, CNVC Certified Trainer

"I enjoyed reading this. I couldn't wait to see what the next story was. I like reading about people being compassionate and soothing conflict instead of escalating. I teach Nonviolent Communication and these will be great examples to go through line by line and see how each participant would respond in that situation."

—JEFF TRETSVEN, Trainer, Coach, Mediator

"Mary's empathy anthology is timely because empathy is needed now more than ever. Reading this can strengthen your compassion muscle and help you find your own voice even during the most difficult interactions. I look forward to sharing these stories with my university students. Kudos, Mary!"

—CHRISTINE KING, CNVC Certified trainer

"I'm so totally delighted with this book, which shares what empathy can look like in a real-life conversation. I've been wanting support for growing this crucial skill and way of being for years, and I believe this book is the answer to this long-lived yearning of mine! Each story seems to capture a different way of being an empathic listener, based upon the people involved and the situation. Perfect! I'm going to draw upon this book for future trainings."

—JANE CONNOR, CNVC Certified Trainer

"I am overjoyed to see this collection of stories of empathy in practice in the real-world conflicts that we are challenged with in our daily lives. This book has something for everyone from compassionate beginner to experienced NVC trainer. I appreciate the care that is shown by selecting stories that not only show the power of empathy, but also show the resulting change that it makes in us as human beings. I will keep this book for my personal growth as well as recommending it for others who are looking to improve their empathy skills and practices."

—DAVID BROWNING, New York City NVC Facilitator

Contents

Empathy at Work:
Creating a Culture of Compassion 97

Empathy in the Community: Caring for Strangers and Neighbors   169

DIVINE EMPATHY—
*Brings divine understanding through
temporary projection or infusion of energies
that allow you to experience (on subtle levels)
patterns that are not necessarily inherent;
facilitates divine perspective-taking without
long-term attachment to the frequencies;
softens your energy to allow for flow
and transformation when stuck
in anger or blame; creates the
feeling of being understood
on deep levels.*

Introduction

Connecting, Learning, and Growing

Marshall Rosenberg, founder of the Center for Nonviolent Communication, often shared in his workshops a story about two warring village chiefs from Nigeria who came together to meet with him after years of escalating violence and murder. Each blamed the other for the mounting bloodshed—a fairly common narrative in our world.

Using the relatively simple process of Nonviolent Communication, Marshall helped shift the conversation, enabling these two antagonists to discover their commonalities. During a single session, one of the chiefs said, "If we could keep talking like this, we wouldn't have to kill each other."

Within a matter of hours, both chiefs went from threats and accusations to acknowledging shared values for equality and safety. Soon after articulating these two needs, along with a few others, they came up with a peace resolution plan for their tribes. How did this happen after years had passed and countless lives had been lost? That is the magic of empathy!

The Power of Stories

When I was first introduced to Nonviolent Communication, it was the stories and anecdotes I heard that stuck with me—and it was these stories that helped me most as I navigated the empathy learning curve in my real-life relationships. Our brains need examples! And good stories help us learn.

As I began to teach Nonviolent Communication to clients and groups, the stories stole the spotlight. They provided real-life examples of how to communicate differently in important conversations. More importantly, perhaps, they provided hope. I began collecting trainers' most teachable stories about empathy and sharing snippets of them for demonstration purposes. I soon realized a book wanted to be birthed. For two years, I sought out the most transformative empathy-based stories I could find, from both seasoned and new Nonviolent Communication practitioners. Some of these inspiring contributions were submitted by those who wanted to remain anonymous, while others have given us permission to acknowledge them and their work, which you can follow if you so choose. A story can, indeed, be the catalyst for a powerful revolution. As you read the seventy-plus stories in this book, you'll encounter new ways to talk to the people in your life. As you revisit the stories over time, you may notice new techniques you might not have seen at first glance; stories can be stealthy that way.

In the end, my wish for you is that your life will be changed, in no uncertain terms, because you see how powerful it can be to lean in toward connection, one conversation at a time.

Helpful Tips

As you read, take note of the wording used in each story to express empathy and mindfulness. Choosing more empathic responses, rather than relying on habitual responses (sometimes called "empathy nots"), can be a powerful way to connect with people and transform conversations. For those wishing to exercise their "empathy muscles," several appendixes provide tips, tools, and more information to guide your learning about the mechanics of the empathy skills used in various stories.

Empathy at Home

Deeper Connections
With Friends and Loved Ones

Marshall Rosenberg, whose name you will see over and again throughout these pages, once said that it may be hardest to give empathy to the people you're closest to.

It's true that we are generally most triggered by those we love: our mothers, fathers, children, lovers, life partners, and best friends. And that's partly why empathizing with them feels out of reach sometimes, especially when there's tension in the air. Learning how to self-regulate or self-manage during triggering conversations is part of what it takes to be empathic. We need self-empathy first before we can show empathy to others. And when you're talking to your meddling father or your depressed teenager, getting self-connected is no small task. Spiritual teacher Ram Dass put it like this: "If you think you're enlightened, go spend a week with your family."

Empathy can be difficult to offer to our loved ones precisely *because* we care about them so much. It can seem unbearable to watch them struggle. We want to help! It's part of our programming to help make the pain of our loved ones go away, so we go into problem-solving, fix-it defaults without even thinking about it—even though what people in pain often want most is to be heard and understood.

3

Empathy requires the ability to witness suffering in others without trying to change it. As soon as you have a thought about what you wish someone would feel or do, you have shifted away from empathy and toward tending to yourself.

One of my mentors says that of all the triggers out there, she struggles the most when her teenage daughter is sad. That's when it's hardest for her to remember to show up empathically, and I can totally relate. It's easier for me to listen and empathize with acquaintances about their health issues, but when a loved one is battling a disease or a good friend is in a miserable job? I want to take action; I want to *do* something. I sometimes can't help squeezing in little pieces of advice, whether they've been requested or not.

We want to help and contribute; it's our natural state and it's a core tenet of Nonviolent Communication. In this section's stories about lovers and loved ones, you'll have the opportunity to see how helpful—and easy—it can be to contribute in the form of deep listening. You'll see how anger and blame get translated into something more connective and productive. You'll hear the words used to repair arguments before they cause painful damage. You'll perhaps notice how loved ones can spontaneously begin to innovate their own solutions to problems upon simply being heard. And you'll get a sense of how self-empathy can transform challenging dynamics in relationships—without having to say anything at all.

*To listen fully means to pay close attention
to what is being said beneath the words.*

—PETER SENGE

A Father's Gift

I was working with a woman named Sandra whose dad was eighty-one years old and thinking about his upcoming death. He wanted Sandra to live in his house after he was gone, but she didn't want to. Although she liked the house, she couldn't live there because when she was alone at night in the house, she was so full of fear—a fear she didn't understand—that she could not sleep there.

They had several conversations about her living in his house, which went nowhere. He tried to convince Sandra, every time she was there, that it was a nice place, a paradise in his words, and that everybody was safe. Sandra was repeatedly stuck when deciding how to respond. She didn't want to lie to him and make promises she couldn't keep, so she was very clear that she would not live there. Whenever she tried to voice her concerns, he redoubled his efforts to give her reasons why it was such a great idea: no rent, really nice place, and an amazing garden.

As I worked with her, I realized a big part of the issue was that she did the exact thing she said her father was doing, which was trying to *explain* herself and *convince* her dad that it simply wasn't possible. We worked together to come up with an alternative way to imagine the conversation.

Here's what it could sound like: "I want to come back to the topic that's been hard for us to talk about. I want to talk about what happens to the house after you die. I've done a lot of thinking. And I want to start by telling you that I finally get it—I get how big the gift is that you're trying to give me. You want my happiness and you want me to live in what you think of as paradise, and I'm very touched. And I want to know if this is what is really motivating you.

"But first I want to tell you what my big problem is. I wish I could receive your gift. Now that I can see how precious and beautiful it is, I wish I could receive it. The thing is, it's not a gift for me in this way. It's not paradise for me. I don't know why. I can't understand why I am always scared when I'm here. If I agree to what you want, it's possible that every night for the rest of my life, I will not sleep well, and I will be scared all night long. I can't imagine this is what you want for me. [*Pause*] I want us to find some other way for this gift to work for me. Are you open to talking about it? Can you see why it can't work for me?"

As we developed this framing, Sandra was able to fully relax and began to smile. The weight was finally being lifted from her. She was ready to speak to her dad with an open heart.

In parting, I would like to quote from Sandra's email to me after her conversation with her dad. It speaks for itself: "I could see the relief in my dad's face when he heard that I finally understood what a treasure he wants to give to me. At the end of the conversation, he said it would be totally fine for him if we rent the house until any of us (me or my boys) would like to live there. I'm still touched! What I didn't expect is that after we came to this place of really hearing each other, my resistance to living in the house decreased a little bit more with every passing day. I can almost imagine buying an alarm system and a big dog and living there . . . but I hope it will not come so soon."

—MIKI KASHTAN, www.thefearlessheart.org

*When we sense ourselves being defensive or
unable to empathize, we need to (1) stop, breathe,
give ourselves empathy; (2) scream nonviolently;
or (3) take time out.*

—MARSHALL B. ROSENBERG, PhD

Falling Into the Pit

*H*ow stupid to even try, I thought. *It's just not a good idea to work together.*

I was in a meeting with my husband to co-develop a workshop we planned to run together. We usually work separately and develop our own programs, but we have a few joint projects. We had gone for a long walk to get inspired. The ideas flowed, we enjoyed each other's creativity, and we built the workshop concept up to the sky.

Some days later, we held a meeting to crunch our enthusiasm-filled ideas into an actual, do-able, time-limited program with defined activities.

As we entered this territory, our moods dropped . . . and dropped . . . and dropped. Our body language became disconnected, then hostile.

I made a few desperate attempts at guessing his feelings and needs. He wasn't buying it. "Don't do that false empathy. It's obvious you don't mean it," he barked, annoyed.

We turned away from each other and tried to continue the

meeting, but we were responding with dry comments to each other's ideas. It didn't feel good. Then—in this pit—we began analyzing and threatening each other.

He began: "You're in a weird mood today. If you don't want to do it, then let's drop it."

"It's not that," I shot back. "I just . . . I don't know . . . since we sat down, you've been so miserable that I can't get enthusiastic. I feel like you hate me!"

"It doesn't have to be perfect, you know," he said, sounding irritated. "Let's just get this done!"

"But . . . I don't know . . ."

"Well, you come up with an idea then. How would you like it to be?"

I felt dread. The energy drained out of me, seeping from my legs into the ground. I glanced sideways at him. He looked jammed up and tense, staring out the window with tight eyes. Hands in his pockets. Shoulders hunched.

I looked at the ground. I felt foggy and gluey and stuck. I told myself nothing creative or joyful or even remotely worthwhile would come out of this. I wondered, in fact, why on earth we worked together because it's the only time we get nearly this miserable. I wished we could kill this project with one blow. I wished I could say that. But I couldn't bring myself to say anything.

There was a long, uncomfortable silence. I thought the silence was my fault and wondered, *Why can't I think of something helpful to say?* The hole I was in got deeper.

He, breaking the silence, said, "This is a waste of time. I could be doing something useful. If you don't want to discuss it . . ."

I interrupted defensively, "I *do* want to discuss it. It's just that . . ." I still couldn't find the words. I just wanted it to be over. To escape this somehow.

How bizarre that moments before we had begun this meeting, this person—my dear husband—seemed so loving and lovable.

And now I only wanted to escape. I hated myself and hated him. A dark mood grew inside me. The inner squeezing grew, like a cramp.

With a flash of inspiration, I burst out of the bottom of my hole and said, "Jackal Gangs! What are your Jackal Gangs doing?"

Jackal Gangs is an idea that came to us in the early stages of our relationship. The "gangs" appeared spontaneously in our conversations and were funny and clarifying. During an especially close phone call once, I found it hard to receive his loving words, so we discovered I could look at my Jackal Gang. They were dressed in yellow protective helmets, standing on small platforms in the middle of a traffic intersection, blowing whistles and furiously pointing with their arms in all directions, trying to control the traffic. By watching them and laughing together, they lost control of me, and I could open again to the marvelous flow of love coming my way.

He replied, "My jackals have their shovels over their shoulders. They are packing up and moving off, muttering about their pay and conditions. They look like a group of road builders. They didn't even want to come to this meeting. I can see now that at the beginning they came in slouching and complaining. They just wanted to go outside and smoke cigarettes and make jokes together."

I listened, perking up, finally interested in and connected with this inner picture he was giving me, which matched my perception of his posture and attitude. It just fit. Inexplicably. I felt back in touch with him. What a relief.

"And yours?" he asked.

"Mine are lying on the floor and trying to get up, but their legs are not strong enough. They keep falling over on top of each other, hurting each other when they fall. Their legs are like rubber and don't hold them up properly. They are wailing and crying out, 'Our legs! What's happened to our legs?!'"

"Do they need some help?" he wondered.

"They want some kind of injection into their legs to firm them up. They need bones to be injected into their legs."

As I spoke this vivid fantasy out loud, I suddenly felt a lot better. Oddly, I felt my own bones firmer in my legs. It was as though I, too, could stand again. I had come out of the pit and noticed there was air to breathe. I took a deep breath.

We looked at each other softly, sadly. Sad that we had become so disconnected. Relieved to be back in loving contact. We hugged quietly for some moments. Then we turned our attention back to the workshop plan and noticed that our usual harmony was restored. Our thoughts began to build on each other's once more, and our plan came together beautifully.

—BRIDGET BELGRAVE, www.liferesources.org.uk

My own time on earth has led me to believe in two powerful instruments that turn experience into love: holding and listening. For every time I have held or been held, every time I have listened or been listened to, experience burns like wood in that eternal fire, and I find myself in the presence of love.

—MARK NEPO

My Whining Kids

A huge issue around my house has always been whining. When I experienced a shift in my perception of the whining, my children were four, seven, and ten.

Before that point, it seemed like they whined all the time. It drove me crazy. Whenever I heard that whiny sound in their voices, I immediately wanted to stop whatever I was doing.

Then I went away to a parenting workshop where I learned that children are just trying to express their needs. After I returned, I noticed that the first time my daughter whined, she was requesting something from me. I suddenly realized that she whined whenever she expected me to reject or deny her request.

I also realized that she was used to having to ask for things and was accustomed to me saying no. It became obvious that, in our interactions, my daughter was often powerless to get something that she wanted.

I felt a huge wave of compassion for my daughter. I saw how

I had not expressed respect for the autonomy needs of my children.

What I had considered whining was their way of trying to be fully heard and to rebel against my lack of respect for their autonomy.

When I realized this, I felt regret and sadness that my relations with my children involved so little trust and respect. I talked with my kids about my thoughts and realizations. I let them know that I very much wanted to listen to them better and to work on growing more trust between us.

"EMPATHY NOTS"
Example

COACHING

"Take a few breaths."
"Here's what you can do . . ."

When I finished, my kids looked at me as though I had come from an alien planet. My four-year-old began to cry. However, within just three weeks of my talk with them, the whining has dramatically decreased, and my children and I have very much enjoyed each other's company.

—Anonymous, Excerpted from the book
Respectful Parents, Respectful Kids

*When one party is in too much pain to hear
the needs of the other, we extend empathy,
taking as long as necessary to ensure that
the person knows their pain is heard.*

—MARSHALL B. ROSENBERG, PhD

Sitting on Opposite Sides of the Couch

The main goal my partner, Jori, and I have as mediators is to cultivate equality and connection between two parties so that compassion is inspired in each of them. In the way we mediate, we don't put any overt attention on coming to specific resolutions. We trust that once people are connected, compassionate giving and receiving will naturally occur, and that solutions will arise organically based on whatever needs are identified during the process.

So on one particular day, we sat with a married couple who were really in a rough patch. They arrived at the mediation separately, at different times. One came into our mediation room and sat on the end of the couch where disputants typically sit. About five minutes later, the other partner arrived. She sat at the opposite end of the couch. They both settled in and leaned away from each other, pressing against their respective armrests. This gave us a lot of information as we gauged their level of connection.

We explained our process and empathized with them right off the bat. We empathized with how it might feel to come to a

13

mediation and to feel so tender and unsure of what would happen next in their relationship.

We began with our usual question: "Who is willing to listen first?"

There was a long silence; nobody really wanted to listen first.

This touches on a really important piece about empathy. Empathy has nothing to do with the words that we say and everything to do with where we put our attention. So Jori and I stayed in that silent space, empathizing with our eyes, with our hearts, with how much these two people both desperately wanted to be understood and heard.

Eventually he said, "I'm willing to listen first." So she proceeded to launch into her story of pain.

We listened to and stayed with her as she spoke. We empathized out loud and reflected back, or recapped, what we heard in terms of what her needs were. At the point when she mentioned one essential need, we said: "We'd like to carry this over to the other person and see if we can get him to reflect it back. Is that okay with you?"

"That would be great," she said.

We repeated the need that we heard her mention, to make it easier for him. Let's just say the need was for understanding. He indicated that he'd be willing to reflect back her need, and he did.

"Thank you." He'd just given us the gift of fulfilling our request, so we expressed our heartfelt gratitude.

Then we asked him, "Now, what feelings are coming up for you?" and he began telling his side of the story.

We listened to him for a while, acknowledging his experience and boiling it down to one essential point, and then did the same thing as before. We asked him for permission to carry over the essential need to his partner, and she was able to reflect it back. We just kept doing this little dance.

It's simple, but we call it a mediation dance. We collect a need from one person and carry it over like a gift on Christmas morning for the other person to unwrap . . . and we find out how it is to receive that need—that gift.

For this couple, the dance went on for around forty-five minutes. If we had recorded it with a video camera, you'd have seen how their bodies stopped leaning away from each other as the process went on. Although their eyes stayed on us—they still refused to look at each other—their bodies began to relax.

After ten more minutes of continued back-and-forth, we watched as they gradually shifted in their seats until their knees pointed toward each other. They still directed most of their comments to us, though, so we kept the process moving forward.

The formula of finding the need and then reflecting it back is almost like a mechanical process. It's really puzzling why it works, but it does! It connects people at the heart. And this couple was no exception.

They gradually, inch by inch, moved toward each other. After fifteen minutes, this husband and wife began talking directly to each other.

Jori and I backed off and let them talk. Within a couple minutes, they were holding hands and had their heads right next to each other, making an A shape. We couldn't hear a word of their conversation, but it didn't matter. They had connected.

They stayed in this cuddling position for at least another ten minutes, which felt almost timeless. It was just so delicious for me and Jori to empathize with their hard-earned connection, after spending so much time empathizing with their pain. It was really beautiful to be in the presence of that extended moment.

Finally, they came back to us and made eye contact, so we continued with the next part of the mediation process. "Who has any ideas about what they'd like to do next?"

They decided they needed to have a meal together—a date. They hadn't had a date in weeks because of the little time they had together in their busy lives. They walked out hand in hand and left one vehicle behind as they drove away together.

That was the first step in a process that strengthened their relationship. It took a few other mediations to clarify some agreements, but they really improved the quality of their connection by empathizing with each other using our support.

This experience gave them a renewed reference point—a reminder of what had been lost when they first started blaming each other. They were able to get past the negative mental image of blaming each other and instead remember the person they fell in love with. To support them through the process and help them move past the pain they'd been stuck in—this was a gift we savored. We always do.

—JIM MANSKE, www.radicalcompassion.com

Empathy is a respectful understanding of what others are experiencing. We often have a strong urge to give advice or reassurance and to explain our own position or feeling. Empathy, however, calls upon us to empty our mind and listen to others with our whole being.

—MARSHALL B. ROSENBERG, PhD

Processing a New Alzheimer's Diagnosis

With my partner still asleep beside me, I stayed in bed one morning because I noticed I was in a funk. A dear friend had been in the hospital, and the trips back and forth to visit her were certainly a little hectic. But something felt really off, and I was having trouble putting my finger on the pulse of it.

I kept thinking about my friend Sherry and how fast her life had gone from normal to complicated. A momentary slip on a wet driveway had led to her needing ankle surgery. The procedure went well, and she'd been released from the hospital, yet her body required the support of a month-long stay at an inpatient rehab facility.

It was depressing and dingy, this rehab place, but her spirits remained quite high. Even though her injuries were purely physical, a lot of people there had suffered from strokes, Alzheimer's, and other maladies affecting cognitive functioning. True to her personality, she used the experience as an "opportunity" and began connecting with everyone she met, learning their stories.

Her attitude was inspiring to me, but I still didn't like that she was there. I began to cry, and hearing me, my partner woke up.

"Hey," he said, "what is it?"

"I've been overwhelmed thinking about this rehab place. The other night, when I was visiting, it was pretty shocking. Sherry seems to be keeping her chin up about being there, but it's disturbing. The hallways are dark. A neighbor was screaming, 'Help me, they've kidnapped me!' the entire time I was there, which is apparently a normal thing. And then a call button alarm at the nurse's station went off for a half hour straight. I went up and said something to the person behind the counter and she responded, 'Yeah, I've gotten used to the sound, so I don't even notice it anymore.' I was appalled and asked, 'But doesn't it mean someone needs something?'"

"Wow," he said, pulling me into a hug. "That's unsettling."

"I just can't stop thinking about my dad ending up in one of those places, with people behind the counter ignoring alerts. I had to tell myself they must be ignoring it for a reason because the lady was so nonchalant, but it was hard to listen to it for so long. I could hear it all the way in Sherry's room!"

"So this takes you to your dad, huh? You're thinking about him in that kind of environment?"

"Yes! It's horrifying!"

The tears really came down. My dad had been diagnosed with Alzheimer's the year before and it was disheartening to visit the hospital, which foreshadowed a potential future for him.

"I mean, I know we're not there yet. And it could be ten more years before we are. But there might come a time when he'll need more care than we can give him at home . . ." I trailed off.

"And you're worried about how that's going to be?" he asked.

"Yes." My mind was all over the place. "I don't feel like I'm doing enough now, honestly. My mom and Stephen and Kathy are taking on the bulk of things. I told myself I'd fly into town every few months to lend a hand—or at least visit—and I haven't. I've only gone twice. It seems so insufficient."

"Feeling guilty? You want to help out more?"

"Yeah. It's hard. I had hoped Kevin would make a trip this past summer. He and I talked about it several times, but it never happened. And I never went, either. I really want to be there while my dad is still himself, so we can connect, you know? We have no idea how long we have. I mean, we talk on the phone all the time, but . . . I don't know."

"So," he said, trying to reflect back, "some of this is about you and your brother Kevin helping out Stephen, Kathy, and your mom back home, and everyone working together. And some of it is just about valuing the time you have left with your dad?"

"Exactly!" I paused for a bit, switching gears. "It reminds me of an Alzheimer's patient I met at the rehab place while eating with Sherry in the TV room. I was working on a jigsaw puzzle and a man came in, muttering and pointing at the puzzle. I had no idea what he wanted, and I couldn't even tell if he was upset or just trying to tell me something. His daughter arrived a few minutes later. We found out he used to be an engineer. As she translated his sounds and gestures, it turned out he was simply trying to give me advice on how to work a puzzle, by doing the edges first. It was heartbreaking! He used to be an engineer!"

We sighed together, lying there, and as more tears spilled, he continued to stay with my nonlinear train of thought.

"Yeah," he said. "It's just painful to think about that kind of loss."

"Yes, it is. That's exactly it." I agreed. "And that wasn't even the worst of it. I forgot to tell you this part. Later on that same trip, I saw a different man who apparently takes off all his clothes every night, strips the sheets off his bed, and runs around. He came out, naked and confused, while I was trying to talk to the glazed-over orderly behind the counter. She had to rush off to help him!"

"Oh my God!" he exclaimed.

"I know. I just can't . . ." I trailed off, not knowing how to finish my sentence.

Taking a breath, he tilted his head and asked, "Is this—everything you're saying—is it about *dignity*? Are you wanting dignity for those patients you've met, and needing to trust that your dad will have a sense of dignity as he declines?"

When he asked me that question, something lifted as one last stream of tears gave way. I felt a huge sense of relief flood my body, like when you finally lie down at the end of a long day.

"Yes, oh my gosh. Dignity . . ." I said, letting my mind sit with this concept. "That's it. I'm worried that he won't be held with dignity by us, or by the orderlies and doctors in the future. Yes. I want my dad's human dignity intact, no matter how he changes. That's totally it. Dignity!"

The conversation soon wrapped up but stayed with me, fresh, for the rest of the week. I was surprised to feel tangible reverberations of relief run through my body each time I reflected on it. A truth was somehow named. I can't explain why it mattered so much to be with this idea of dignity, this mantra, this promise to my dad. But it did. It mattered.

—MARY GOYER, www.consciouscommunication.co

Listening creates a holy silence.
When you listen generously to people, they can
hear truth in themselves, often for the first time.
And in the silence of listening, you can know
yourself in everyone. Eventually you may be able
to hear, in everyone and beyond everyone, the
unseen singing softly to itself and to you.

—RACHEL NAOMI REMEN

Being With My Teenager's Heartbreak

Here's one of the questions I often pose when teaching parenting classes: "Where do you have a hard time with your kid having a hard time?"

I recently asked myself this same question after returning home from a five-day work trip. My sixteen-year-old was in a bad mood, and I initially thought it was about me. But I made eye contact with her and watched as she slumped down on the couch, saying, "Everything's bad."

I could already feel the urge to reassure her or talk her out of it, even though she hadn't mentioned any details. Instead I said gently, "Well, what is it? What do you want me to know?"

She hesitated, but as she told her story, I understood that she felt left out by friends who were spending more time with each other than with her. There were so many times during this halted story that I felt the impulse to jump in and tell her: "Oh, they totally adore you. They love you."

Or I could've given her advice like, "Well, have you asked them this or that?"

But I somehow managed to hold my tongue and not give unsolicited advice or unrequested reassurance. Instead, I stuck to the basics—reflection (recapping), empathy, and plain old listening.

One thing I said was, "So when they go off at fourth period and spend time together, it sounds like you end up feeling lonely, you know? Do you wish they knew how much you miss them, but maybe it feels a little bit too vulnerable to say that?"

She softened and cried. "Yeah, it's like I feel stuck. I can't really express anything to them. I can't say anything to them because they'd just blow it off."

What also came out was that she had tried to express her concern to several other friends, but they had given her either advice or reassurance, and she was so discouraged that they didn't seem to really hear her.

By the end of the twenty minutes that we sat together, she had both laughed and cried. She said she felt some relief, and she thanked me for listening. I felt close to her and she felt heard. I had averted reinforcing the idea that nobody was listening, which she had experienced with her friends.

I also realized that if I had assumed she was mad at me, I may have cut her off at the very beginning, which would've been such a missed opportunity. Instead, I met her where so many of us have been: feeling left out, wanting to know that we matter and belong, and that our friends adore us. I would have missed something really sweet.

—KRISTIN MASTERS, www.nvcsantacruz.org

Empathy is the strongest antidote for shame.

—BRENÉ BROWN

Self-Empathy for Shame

One of the most difficult emotions for humans to experience is shame. It produces the greatest flow of cortisol, the stress hormone, of any human feeling. Mostly people try to avoid shame, using distraction or addiction strategies to shift their brain chemistry enough to pop out of the experience. Alcohol, for example, is a great shame neutralizer. "Bottoms up!"

Every year I experience a movement into shame so great and so persistent (it lasts for four weeks!) that I have begun to mark the time on my calendar in an effort to anticipate what's happening and to give myself extra support. The time period is October 20 through November 12. As near as I can tell, my mom had a difficult time during this period, so I imagine she went into a dark place during these weeks every year of my childhood. It just happens (coincidentally? I don't know) to span the creation of Halloween costumes, my birthday, and end the day after my parents' wedding anniversary.

In the past couple of years, I've been focusing on the question of what deep needs our nervous systems are meeting by creating self-sabotaging behaviors. To ask this question, we need to stop thinking of ourselves as alone. We have to strip away the myth of aloneness and look at the original dyads we were a part of.

Humans are not grown in petri dishes, they are made inside wombs and relationships.

As I evolve in the work I do with others, bringing empathy processes to heal and transform difficult emotional experiences, I try the work out on myself. So this year I asked myself, where is the missing dyad partner in my shame? And what needs am I meeting with the shame? I opened my sensation gate to let in what my body is feeling. What came to mind was a deep loneliness and a sense of the absolute disappearance of my mother's warmth and her shift to cold, mechanical functionality.

As I brought a sense of the missing person in the shame dyad, my perception was that I was receiving scrutiny and dismissal. My mother moved far away from me in my imagination, increasing my sense that I was in this on my own. The density of the shame lightened when I allowed myself to wonder if she was leaving her child self behind with me, and if I might be feeling the shame for both of us. Her father turned away from her when she was eight and she never saw him again, but she asked to be buried with him when she died. I had an image of peeling orphan after orphan from past generations off my shame body and letting them stand around me in acknowledgment of the loss of parents.

My shame was lighter, not so dense, but there was a nausea in my head.

My body's vow to me was something like "I, Sarah's body, solemnly swear to you, my essential self, that I will keep my head and my eyes down for the rest of my life so that my presence doesn't burden others who do not want me in order to save myself from heartbreak and disappointment and further shame, and not to be in relationship with the planet itself in order to lessen the burden I place on the earth and on life, no matter the cost to myself." Ugh. Lots of nausea there.

And then I asked myself, "Sarah's essential self, did you hear the vow that Sarah's body made to you?"

24

My essential self said, "Yes, although the voice is very small and weak and doesn't have much life energy in it, I heard it."

"Is that a good vow for Sarah's body?"

"No, definitely not."

"Would you tell her that you release the vow?"

"Sarah's body, I release you from this vow and I revoke this contract. I wish for you to know that the world delights in your existence. I wonder if you were so worried that you were broken and defective? Do you need to know that you are just right? I wish for you to reach out for and enjoy relationship."

As my body experienced the release of the vow, my head came up, creating shooting pains at the base of my skull as the muscles there let go and started to move. My shoulders came down, and an encasement of tension that had surrounded my whole body faded.

I was meeting deep needs for humility, integrity, and respect with my strategy—my vow to pull myself back from life in order to hold everyone else with care. And I was making myself safe from disappointment at the same time. But that wasn't a particularly good strategy for a lifetime.

The shame and the nausea are gone now. The period of shame had been such a lifelong experience, it was impossible to imagine that things could really be different. But I'm willing to wait and see where I can bring empathy to bear next in my ongoing quest for self-warmth and self-care.

—SARAH PEYTON, www.yourresonantself.com

> *We hone our skills to hear the need within every*
> *message, even if at first we have to rely on guesses.*
>
> —MARSHALL B. ROSENBERG, PhD

Averting a New Year's Eve Fight

One New Year's Eve a few years back, I saw firsthand the simple yet almost miraculous transformative power of empathy, which inspired me to sign up for several trainings to learn as much as I could about the process and principles.

My wife and I had gone to a quiet evening dinner with another couple and came home around 9:00 p.m. We live close to the downtown area, where there is always a festive atmosphere on New Year's, and we could hear the voices and shouts of people as they congregated.

We spent some time together, talking about the enjoyable evening with our friends. After a while my wife said she was tired and ready for bed. I relaxed as she got ready for bed, still able to hear the revelers in the streets downtown. As she pulled out a book and climbed into bed, I told her I was going to check out the scene downtown. I'm fairly extroverted—I love parties and being around lots of people, so walking around downtown seemed like the perfect thing to do. I could watch people and perhaps run into friends.

"Why do you always have to go out?" she asked, clearly annoyed. "Can't you ever just stay home?"

I felt my whole body tense up. I love going out. I feel enlivened when I'm around people. My wife and I had a nice day and evening together. She was in bed and would be asleep soon. I couldn't see any reason why I shouldn't go out. What was the alternative? Stay home doing nothing?

A short pause gave me just enough time to inquire if there might be something else going on besides her judgment that I always need to go out and can never just stay at home.

It wasn't easy, though. Almost every fiber in my being interpreted her comments as false . . . I don't *always* need to go out. I also felt like it was a total disaster for my prospects of living a happy life. I was married to a woman who was painfully and harshly judgmental about a choice of mine that seemed innocent! Not to mention that being out with people is a deep, authentic expression of something that gives me joy.

All of this was boiling inside, but I managed to stay calm.

"Can you say more?" I asked.

She repeated, "You always need to go out. You just can't ever stay home."

Ugh. *Keep going. Don't give up,* I told myself.

"Can you tell me more about what's going on for you? What are you needing?" I asked.

Twice she repeated that I always need to go out, and then she said something new.

"I'm not feeling well, and I don't want to be alone! I want someone to be with me and take care of me!!"

"Oh!" So that's what she was asking for!

Even though I was still triggered by her initial statements, when I heard what she wanted, my immediate response was to want to take care of her. It superseded my desire to go downtown and be part of the festivities.

So I stayed home, a bit shaken by the route we had taken to get to that moment, but happy to show her my love when she didn't feel well or want to be alone. She just wanted some care. Being able to translate her words made such a difference.

—ANONYMOUS

*When you plant lettuce, you don't blame the lettuce if it does not
grow well. You look into the reasons why it is not doing well.
It may need fertilizer, or more water, or less sun. You never
blame the lettuce. Yet if we have problems with our friends or
our family, we blame the other person. But if we know how to
take care of others, they will grow well, just like the lettuce.
Blaming has no positive effect at all, nor does trying to persuade
by means of reason or argument. That is my experience.
No blame, reasoning, no argument—just understanding.
If you understand, and you show that you understand,
you can love, and any difficult situation will improve.*

—THICH NHAT HANH

Shifting Blame and Criticism

Carla came to me because she thought her daughter should be paying more attention to her own daughter—Carla's beloved granddaughter. She thought her daughter, Julia, was being a selfish, bad mother. Wiping her eyes, Carla told me she was afraid her granddaughter suffered from neglect and that it would affect her entire life. She shook her head in disbelief and described how Julia ignored Sarah and never made time to play with her.

Using the No-Fault Zone Game, I gave Carla the red card deck and asked her to find the cards that described her feelings. With tears flowing, she carefully placed several cards on her mat: Disappointed, Hurt, Discouraged, Worried, Anxious, Helpless, and Hopeless.

"How can my daughter be so out of touch?" she sobbed.

"As you think about that, a lot comes up, huh?" I asked.

"Mmm-hmm. It's so sad."

"Well, let me ask you this. What do you want most in this situation?" I asked as I handed her the yellow Needs card deck.

There was a long pause. She thought about what she wanted Julia to do, and especially all the ways she wanted her to change. She remembered how Julia repeatedly pushed her away and told her she didn't want any more advice.

Eventually, Carla focused on herself and realized that what she wanted most was to be heard. She was missing a connection with her daughter and wanted to feel close to her again.

Carla stopped crying and was visibly calmer. I moved the game mat to her left.

"What do you think Julia's feelings are about this situation?" I asked, placing a different game mat on the table in front of her. I handed her another Feelings card deck. She chose Frustrated, Stressed, and Hurt, and placed them on her new mat. She continued rifling through the deck.

Seeing the Lonely and Scared cards, she stopped. With a furrowed brow, she turned to me. "Do you think she's lonely and scared because we aren't getting along?"

As she glanced between her own mat of Feelings cards and back to Julia's, her brow relaxed. Something was clearly stirring in her.

I passed her a Needs card deck and asked, "What do you think Julia wants most right now?"

She shuffled through the cards and pulled out Understanding, Love, Caring, and Kindness, arranging them carefully on the mat. Searching through the deck again, she saw To Be Heard and stopped abruptly. "That's it! She wants to be heard."

With tears streaming she whispered, "She wants the same thing I do. I can't believe how out of touch with her I have been."

—VICTORIA KINDLE HODSON, www.thenofaultzone.com

Empathy allows us to "re-perceive"
[our] world in a new way and go on.

—MARSHALL B. ROSENBERG, PhD

Getting to Forgiveness

I experienced a lot of physical violence from my dad when I was a kid. I have painful memories of being hit and dragged, of seeing my parents yelling and slapping each other in the face. I often sat at the kitchen counter, trying to make sense of it and feeling scared and confused. For the longest time, I couldn't understand or put into words how I felt about my dad.

I remained angry and hurt for years, and as an adult I began to realize how much these experiences had affected me. I wanted to heal, so I journaled and went to counseling and twelve-step meetings. But I also avoided my dad.

In the space I took for myself, I wrote a lot and practiced self-empathy. It dawned on me that I didn't want to say I was abused, neglected, or misunderstood, because those types of labels kept me feeling stuck and helpless. Instead, I connected to how hurt I felt because I wanted more support and care from my dad. I was angry because my needs for safety and protection were not met on many occasions. I felt disappointed because I wanted respect and consideration, even as a little kid. I was frustrated because I was desperate to be heard and understood. I felt sadness because I needed to know I was valued, celebrated, and loved as a kid.

I repeated this type of internal dialogue to myself over
and again, and as it soaked in over time, I began to open up to
forgiveness for my dad. Through reflection and prayer, I saw
how my needs had an inherent beauty to them. They pointed to
something in my heart, even in the midst of the violence, that
spoke of God's love for me.

In his last days, I had an opportunity to talk to him about
everything. We had an honest conversation from a place of love
and compassion, which was possible because I had already
forgiven him in my heart.

Dad had spent the end of his life hospitalized with a lung
disease. When I first visited his hospital room, I tried to hide
my feelings and act strong, like I thought a man should. I soon
realized it was taking too much energy to fake strength, so I
decided to be fully present instead. I cried, letting my tears flow
when they came. I think this kind of emotional honesty was new
for him, but I was relieved to be myself. And it seemed that my
father was able to accept me, and my honesty, during our visits.
This vulnerability gave us the opportunity to reminisce about the
good times we had together and for me to share my gratitude with
him for the many ways he'd truly supported me as a kid.

During one of these talks, my dad asked for more oxygen. I
paused for a moment and found the courage to say, "Dad, we're
giving you all we've got. We can't turn it up any more."

He didn't say anything and neither did I. We knew he was
getting close to transitioning.

Later that day, the doctor examined him and said, "If you were
meaning to have any conversations, now is the time."

I was the only visitor that afternoon, so I settled in to talk
with him, just the two of us. There was one thing I wanted to
bring up. I took his hand and said, "Dad, I have some regret about
my distance from you after your divorce from Mom. I'm sad that
we lost so much time. I was confused and needed space to figure
things out."

"I'm sad about that too," he said. "That was a really difficult time."

He also shared one of his regrets with me, while struggling to breathe. "When you were younger, I wish I had been more loving."

I said, "Dad, I forgive you for all that, I really do."

He nodded, his face pained behind his oxygen mask. I cried while we sat together quietly.

I am grateful to have spent the last two weeks of my dad's life with him. A part of me healed as we talked. I felt torn between the joy of connecting with him and sadness that I had waited so long. I mourn that he is no longer here to talk with me, hang out, and hug.

My experience of forgiving him has given me a sense of peace and calm around our relationship, as if the healing extended into the past, bringing restoration to my heart. I hope he's hearing my words, so he can celebrate how far we came during our time together. Thanks, Dad!

—JAMES PRIETO, www.compassionateconnecting.com

*Listen to what people are needing
rather than what they are thinking.*

—MARSHALL B. ROSENBERG, PhD

Housemate Clashes

I've been lucky to live with several amazing housemates in the expensive San Francisco Bay Area. We started as strangers and became friends. We cooked together, swapped rides to the airport, and casually shared everyday moments. I couldn't understand why anyone would prefer living alone to having that kind of built-in support system.

In my early thirties, I met Molly and we decided to room together. Despite my slight uneasiness during our first weeks together, I wasn't too worried. Was it my imagination, or did she seem a little territorial with her things? I had lived with a lot of people by then. I'd always found that once we settled on the chore wheel, shower logistics, and guest sleepover details, the rest took care of itself.

Things between us never did settle, though. Molly often seemed on edge, and our everyday communications were strained. We could usually smooth things out, but it took effort. After several months together, I noticed I was avoiding her more and more. It felt easier. But it didn't leave a lot of "capital" in the connection bank for us to draw from when we eventually ran into bigger challenges.

I had always prided myself in my ability to get along with almost anyone, but I found I had a short fuse for certain types of interactions with Molly. One day I nearly blew up when I saw a note from her about a living room loveseat I had just donated to a teacher's classroom. The note said: "Bummed the chair is gone. Now there's nowhere comfortable to sit."

Seriously? I fumed for a solid five minutes. Then I took a deep breath, reminded myself of the "difficult conversation" fundamentals I often taught clients, and went looking for her to see if she had a second to talk. Her face looked hard, she nodded with no hint of a smile, and I had to take another breath. I knew she was one of my biggest teachers during that time, so I had to actively remind myself to come back into the space of compassion I wanted to stay anchored in.

"Um," I started tentatively, "so I'm looking at this note. It looks like you might be upset. You wish I hadn't given away the chair?"

"Yeah!" she replied. "Now I don't have anywhere to sit. I don't like the new chair and that sofa isn't comfortable, either. So I can't be comfortable in our living room."

"Mmm. Okay, so the sofa doesn't work for you? And the new chair isn't comfy for you like the old one was?" I confirmed.

"It's not. And now things look totally stark in there. It's changed the room."

"So there's an aesthetic piece too. You're not happy with how the new furniture looks."

"No! Look at it! I mean . . ." She threw up her hands.

"All right. So you're kind of hating the change all around."

"Yes!" she said with an exasperated voice. "I come home and it's just gone!"

"Mmm-hmm, got it. Sounds like . . . I'm wondering if it has to do with wanting to feel good in your own house?" I asked.

"Look, yes. I'm also just fried from work. There's some hard stuff going on there and I'm a little stressed." She sighed deeply and her shoulders sank down.

"Mmm," I nodded. "Okay, so there's also work stress in the mix." She nodded and sighed again. After a moment of space, I shifted gears a bit. "The thing is, I'm a little confused. We talked about getting rid of the loveseat two or three times before I did it. I told you I wanted to replace the dingy old thing with something fresh, and I got your feedback on colors for the new piece. Later, you asked how the old one would be transported away. So I really thought you were clear on my plans . . ."

"Well, I didn't know it would happen so fast!" she blurted out.

"Okay." I breathed and closed my eyes for a second. I really wanted to finish my thought, but I tried to go back to her. "You were a little shocked."

"Exactly," she declared.

I waited to see if there was more, but she looked at me expectantly. I tried to find my train of thought.

"I'm confused because I thought we'd talked a few times about this chair. You didn't mention any concerns, as I recall. Now you're surprised and upset, and I'm a little baffled. Do you see how I could be a bit confused right now?"

"Well, I didn't know this would happen right now. Why do you have to make changes when I'm moving out in a few months? Can't you just wait?"

Now it was my turn to be surprised. She wanted me to wait for her to move out? She had been making tentative moving plans and then canceling them for some time. I felt a clear *no* running through my body. Still, I tried to connect with her.

"Okay, so you'd really like certain things to be settled for a while? To have some calm or continuity? Am I close?" I asked, not feeling very sure.

"Well, it's just that so many things are up in the air for me right now. I'm trying to make a lot of things happen, so yes, I want things to stay the same. I want to feel at home here."

"Got it. Like a little sanctuary."

"Yeah," said Molly, looking more settled.

"Okay, I hear that. I'd like for our home to be like that for both of us, and I'm happy to keep asking for your feedback when I'm about to do something in our common space. But it would be a real stretch for me to stop my beautifying project. I've been living with old or cheap things for so long, and it means a lot to me to be able to afford some nicer pieces that match. Do you mind telling me what you're getting from what I'm saying, just so I know I'm coming across the way I'm trying to?" I asked.

"Um, sure. It feels good for you to be decorating," she said.

"Right, that's a chunk of it." I nodded. "And I also want to be clear, I'm not trying to make changes underneath your nose. I don't mind hearing your opinions about my ideas because I want our place to feel good for you too. Does that make sense?"

"I think so."

"Okay. I'm sorry it was startling for you to come home to a new chair. I don't see things I want to buy very often, so I don't expect much to change in the next few months. But I do want to keep my eye out in case I stumble on something I love."

"Okay, sure. Could you just let me know if you're planning on moving something big out here?" she asked.

"No problem," I said, relieved.

There was nothing magical about our resolution. I still felt exasperated. In fact, for days I wanted to remind her how she hated the old chair, how it was *her* choice to keep the uncomfortable sofa, and that I'd wanted a new sofa since the beginning.

Still, we both felt mostly heard and we had softened through the course of the conversation. For us, it was good enough.

—ANONYMOUS

This is the work of compassion:
to embrace everything clearly without imposing
who we are and without losing who we are.

—MARK NEPO

Talking About Sex

Pat and Chris had been working on their sexual relationship because, like many couples, talking about sex often triggered fear, guilt, or shame for them. They both struggled with beliefs like: *Saying no to having sex with my partner is wrong. I should want to when they want to. My partner will pull away from me if I don't have sex when they ask. When my partner says no to having sex with me, I think I'm not lovable, not attractive, or not good enough.*

So one day, Pat and Chris approached a tender conversation with extra kindness and gentleness.

Pat began: "I want to connect with you about what's going on for both of us around sex in our relationship. Would you be willing to take an hour or so to talk about what's up for both of us, and see what we both want?"

Chris took some time before replying, "Honestly, I feel nervous because I really want acceptance and understanding, not pressure. Or blame, for that matter. So yes, I'm up for that, but would you be willing to pause if I ask for it, wherever we are in the conversation?"

"Sure!" Pat replied. "Yes, I'll pause for a break when you ask, or when I feel like I could use it. I also want you to know that I'm not feeling angry. What's most important to me is that each of us is

37

taking care of ourselves in our relationship. I support you in doing what's best for you. Can you tell me what you heard?"

"Yep, I got that you will pause when asked. That you're not mad, and that you support me in doing what's best for me. It's important to you that we are taking care of ourselves in our relationship."

Pat and Chris made some explicit agreements, including using mindfulness breaks, taking things in small chunks, and trying to listen without cross talk or problem solving.

"Here's what's up for me," began Pat. "It's been a little over a month since we had sex. I'm feeling sad because I miss that connection and closeness with you. Can you tell me what you heard there?"

Chris replied, "I heard you say you want to have more sex."

Pat took a deep breath. *I want to stay true to the process. Don't defend. Don't accuse Chris of not listening. Try it again, maybe more concisely this time.*

"EMPATHY NOTS"
Example

REASSURANCE

"I'm sure it's not that bad."
"Don't worry."

"Thanks for telling me what you heard." Another breath. "What I really want you to get is my sadness in missing a closeness with you. Would you be willing to try reflecting what you're hearing again?"

"Okay," Chris replied. "You miss feeling close to me."

"Yes, exactly. I'm also feeling curious and wanting to understand you. What comes up for you when you think about us having sex?"

Chris paused and then answered, "I feel tense to begin with. And I have a feeling that I 'should' have sex, which creates even more tension for me. If I'm not feeling relaxed, connected, and trusting, it's really hard for me to access any sexual desire. What did you hear there?"

Pat reflected back, still focused on breathing, "I heard that you feel you 'should' and that you have some tension. You need relaxation, connection, and trust. So when you're tense, it's hard to feel sexy. Did I get it?"

"Yes, thanks. I don't know why I'm so tense. It's really frustrating for me."

"Uh-huh, feeling frustrated. You wish you had some clarity about where that tension and mistrust come from?"

Chris visibly relaxed. "Yeah."

"Well, it seems like we could take our time here and see if any clarity pops up for you. I could just sit here quietly and offer empathy as something more comes up. Or we could talk about what we can do differently to help meet your needs for relaxation, connection, and trust. What do you think?"

"Right now, the second one sounds better—talking about what we can do differently. I've given some thought to what might help with trust and connection."

"Okay, great. I'd love to hear it!" exclaimed Pat.

"One idea is just accepting me as I am by acknowledging my feelings when I'm upset or worried, rather than giving me advice or telling me not to worry about it. For example, just saying something like, 'Yeah, that's scary for you,' or 'I can see how that would be hard,' goes a long way for me. You know, like you are doing right now. Would you be willing to focus on that for the rest of the week?" Chris asked.

Pat felt an impulse to talk about all the times he had done that and spent another moment breathing—aware that a defensive response could break the vulnerable connection—before answering carefully.

"I would like to do that. I know when you're upset, I just want to make it better. I try to solve things or console you, and I get that it's disconnecting for you. I commit to just offering empathy for the rest of this week. Can we check in about it on Friday after dinner?"

"Yes," said Chris. "Just hearing you mention touching base

on Friday is a relief. I can see how much effort you're putting into this. I see you worked to stay connected in our conversation and it gives me hope that we can face challenges together in a way that works. Thank you."

"Ahh." Pat smiled and exhaled. "You're relieved and you appreciate that I'm doing what I can to make this conversation work?"

"Exactly! And I'm thinking about the intimacy you're missing. I wonder if it would nourish your need for closeness if I offer a hug, fully inhaling and exhaling together, a kiss, and a few moments of eye-gazing each time we come together at home after being apart?"

Pat looked up with bright eyes and happily replied, "Wow, that would be so nourishing for me! Thank you!"

—LASHELLE LOWE-CHARDÉ, www.wiseheartpdx.org

*Empathic connection involves connecting with
what is alive in the other person at this moment.*

—MARSHALL B. ROSENBERG, PhD

Tiny Healing Hands

I hadn't asked anyone to join me. To me, being capable meant going it alone. It was hard enough to acknowledge needing support, but even more difficult to ask for it.

In the medical office I read every line of paperwork, much to the nurse's surprise. I caught the part about leaving a metal tag in my breast. "To mark the spot," it said. I declined. See? I could do it by myself.

The procedure was called a core-needle biopsy. My doctor wanted to be sure a lump she found in my breast was benign. I took the wording literally. Needles are tiny, like the ones in sewing kits, and I prepared myself for a pinprick.

As I lay on the medical table, and the doctor hovered over me, I became deeply aware of my aloneness. I vowed to never "go it alone" again, at least for any medical procedure. I decided that doing things solo did not provide evidence for anything about my capability or strength. It only left me feeling lonely. Soon after my solitude sunk in, I realized this was no familiar needle. It was quite big and the doctor tried to hide it from my view, a tactic he likely developed after experiencing reactions from other patients.

He turned on the needle, which buzzed like an electric carving knife for a holiday turkey. I could feel the tug as this machine

41

entered and exited my breast, taking a core of tissue I later learned was the diameter of a number two pencil. The saving grace here was that the procedure was quick and the results were benign.

After the ordeal, I drove to a friend's place for a planned friend-date. On the way there, I realized I was in shock, terrified beneath my skin and my neutral face. But I did things alone, you know? So I kept moving. I walked through her door, without having processed a single emotion, and stepped into the joyous chaos of my friend's young household.

Their two-year-old, Ezra, was running around in his pajamas, his curly hair bouncing above curious eyebrows and his baby brown eyes. He noticed me, greeted me in his toddler way, then chuckled as he ran off. Ready for some stillness, I found a big comfy recliner in a corner and as I settled into it, I began to cry.

My body began touching into the fear and the loneliness I'd felt at the doctor's office, lying on that table, and I felt something stir from deep within. It surprised me. However, since there was a child in the room, I was sensitive to keep my reactions low-key so he wouldn't be startled or confused. He couldn't have known what started my tears. Ezra was absorbed in his imagination, doing his Tasmanian devil toddler moves, smiling and being himself.

Ezra usually does his own thing after I arrive. This time, however, after my tears had passed, Ezra approached me. Not capable of many words, let alone sentences, he put his hands on my knees and stood there. I can still remember the palms of his two-year-old hands on my skin. Though he'd never placed his hands on me before, Ezra—this toddler priest—held them steady for what seemed like an eternity. He looked right into my eyes, holding what I received as gentle curiosity.

It was as though this little being was drawn to my hurt. His tiny healing hands conveyed warmth. My nervous system calmed, and I felt seen. I did not need to detail to this little spirit the personal tragedy of my day, my choices, regrets, and terror. The moment with him was enough, simple but powerful.

42

I felt the deep accompaniment reach my core. Suddenly, he laughed and shifted back into his two-year-old world. It was the curiosity, presence, and connection Ezra demonstrated that still touches me. Little Ezra now struts around as a fifteen-year-old high schooler. His heart is just as big as it always was, and mine is a little bigger because of him.

—SHEILA MENEZES, www.compassionatereturn.com

*Eventually I learned to translate
my judgments into feelings and needs
and to give myself empathy.*

—MARSHALL B. ROSENBERG, PhD

Dating, Self-Love, and
Transcending Rejection

The phrase "thin-skinned" fails to capture the intense emotional highs and lows I often experience, particularly in romantic relationships. It's especially painful when I think I'm being rejected or abandoned, ideas that usually unleash an onslaught of near-crippling self-doubt, anger, and distress.

As a student of Nonviolent Communication, I have listened to Marshall Rosenberg's CDs and watched his videos on YouTube countless times. I have practiced his strategies of empathy toward myself, feeling awe and conviction about the transformative power of such a simple notion as "self-empathy."

I experienced this transformative power firsthand after Tom, a man I dated for four months, suddenly ceased all communication with me. This brief relationship challenged me incredibly. I tended to put his needs way above mine. I felt needy and codependent, due in part to my father's death while we dated. And I was especially triggered when I faced his rejection after feeling particularly open and receptive to him.

It had started out well enough, with me putting my hopes on the line. I said, "I know we're not exclusive. I like you and I enjoy spending time with you. I'd like to know if you're seeing someone else or if you feel the same."

Tom replied, "I feel the same. I'm not interested in anyone else. But I'm concerned that I may not be able to spend enough time with you. I've got a lot going on and things will be full for several months because I'm trying to get my business up and running."

We agreed to continue seeing each other at least once a week. I felt encouraged and gratified that I had confronted my discomfort to share what I really wanted with Tom, and that he had responded in such a receptive and equally honest way. I was thrilled.

After we spent the night together for the first time, Tom didn't reach out to me for weeks. I didn't make any immediate assumptions, but a few weeks stretched into months of non-responsiveness. It was painful, but I stayed present with myself as a range of emotions swept over me: surprise, confusion, anger, and sadness. One way that I comforted myself was by watching videos and reading articles about "ghosting," which is ending a relationship by vanishing into thin air without any communication. Learning how common the practice of ghosting is helped me loosen the stranglehold of taking the rejection so personally, as an indictment of me being unlovable and undesirable.

Still, I felt anger toward Tom. I navigated this turbulence by asking myself how I felt and what I needed. I needed honesty, more from myself than anyone else. Although I felt disappointed and sad, I also felt tremendous relief that Tom had decided to break off contact when he did. I would have felt like emotional roadkill if he had waited until my feelings for him grew stronger before severing connection.

As I continued to check in with myself, I noticed another familiar pattern: I was comparing myself with other imaginary women. There is little that stings more than going down the rabbit hole of insecurity and angst induced by thoughts of being less attractive, appealing, or interesting than someone else. I tried to keep it real by reminding myself that even if Tom was distracted by other women, it wasn't a reflection on my value or what I have to offer. It was simply about one person making a choice.

While this empathy process wasn't easy or pain-free, it was far from the devastating experience I'd expected. In fact, it left me feeling more emboldened to articulate my needs to those I care about, and to be more respectful of others' choices that don't match my preferences. In honoring myself in all these ways, I gave myself a much greater sense of internal love and worthiness than any form of external validation has ever provided.

—MARY ROAF

If we find ourselves unable or unwilling to empathize despite our efforts, it is usually a sign that we are too starved for empathy to be able to offer it to others.

—MARSHALL B. ROSENBERG, PhD

Connecting With My Mom

My relationship with my mom had been strained since I entered adulthood. It consisted of a phone call once a month or so, in which she told me what I should be doing, and I told her what she should be doing. The conversations weren't very long, and we were definitely not connecting.

After I had completed a year or so of intensive Nonviolent Communication training, I moved into a Zen monastery. With the support of this focused environment, it came to me that perhaps I could change the dynamic with my mom if I just offered empathy for everything she expressed. I knew this wouldn't be easy, so I put some safety measures around it. I would only call when I was feeling clear-minded and emotionally equipped to handle it. I would get off the phone the moment I veered away from empathy. I would aim to call once a week.

Before my first call, I reflected on the types of things my mom said that I reacted to, so I could prepare a new conversational pathway.

The next time we spoke, it didn't take long before we went into some familiar themes.

"Why do you want to live in a monastery?" she asked. "You spent all that money on school and you're not making use of it."

I replied, "Confusing, huh? I'm guessing you want to know that I have security and everything I need. Is that right?"

"Well, yes. So why aren't you working?" she continued.

"Sounds like you're worried about me."

"Yes," she said. There was an awkward pause, then an immediate subject switch. "Can you check on your sister? She won't call me back."

I could have given a direct answer, but I knew this was a layered subject. I asked, "It's scary when you don't know where she is and what she's doing, huh?"

"Yes, can you go check on her tomorrow?"

"Hmm, you really want some way to connect with her and know she is safe. Is that it?"

And so it went. At some point during these calls, I would start defending my decisions and as soon as I heard myself doing that, I got off the phone. My mom didn't know what to do with the empathy at first. There were awkward pauses and her sounding frustrated, saying things like, "Why won't you answer me?!" I don't think she felt any more connected to me at first. For me, the results were immediate. I felt so much more alive and loved interacting with her in this way. I was relating with integrity and it was satisfying. But it was still difficult.

Months went by with me calling her once a week and offering empathy. Incrementally, I could hear a softening in her tone, which I interpreted as her heart opening to me. Slowly she gave up on her "shoulds" for me more easily.

Somewhere around the six-month mark, something new happened. She gave me the usual order to go check on my sister because she hadn't heard from her. I responded with empathy as I had many times over the months, feeling her pain with her and letting it live in our interaction. Then for the first time in my life, I heard my mom express a feeling.

"Yeah, it really hurts," she said. I froze as though a precious little bird had just alighted next to me.

Ever so gently I said, "I know it does. It hurts a lot."

Slowly, she expressed more feelings during our calls. Along with that emotional expression came genuine curiosity about my life and what was meaningful for me, something I had longed for over the years. I remember clearly the first moment she asked about my life in an authentic way even though it was fifteen years earlier.

She asked, "Are you happy living at the monastery?"

"Yeah, Mom," I said.

"Okay, as long as you're happy," she acknowledged.

My mom and I enjoy a sweet and mutual love and respect these days. We talk on the phone often, and I visit her several times a year. She has let me know that I'm the only person in her life to whom she can tell anything.

—LASHELLE LOWE-CHARDÉ, www.wiseheartpdx.org

Their goal becomes providing the empathic connection and education that will enable them to transcend their violence and engage in cooperative relationships.

—MARSHALL B. ROSENBERG, PhD

A Hit Instead of a Kiss

I was visiting my son, who has two boys of his own, and was preparing to say goodbye at the end of the visit. As I leaned over to say goodbye and kiss my two-year-old grandson, he hit me in the face.

I was shocked and stood there, still. Immediately my son swooped up my grandson, held him, and said, "You're sad to see your grandma go?"

My grandson started crying and said, "Yes, I don't want her to go!"

My son replied, "I hear you're sad and don't want her to go, but hitting her isn't the way to say that, honey."

He used a sweet and tender voice as he patted my grandson's back. "I know you're sad. I know you don't want her to go but, in our family, we don't hit when we're upset. We use our words."

He was totally present with my grandson, just being with him without any punitive mind-set. He was with both of us as he reached out, put his hand on my shoulder, and said: "Mom, how about you? Are you okay?"

"Well, yes," I replied. "Just surprised. I wasn't expecting to get a hit instead of a kiss."

He was emphatically present with me and his son in the same moment. How fortunate my grandsons are to have him for a father.

—MAIR ALIGHT, www.mairalight.com

Without connection to feelings and needs,
advice is just another piece of floating information
in an already overwhelmed person.

—*LASHELLE LOWE-CHARDÉ*

New Approach to Helping Her Kids

A t the beginning of our third class together, a woman named Nancy, who was incarcerated in the county jail, said she had a very upsetting phone call with her son, Ray. After a big fight with his wife, he had moved out of the house.

"My marriage is over," Ray declared to his mother on the phone.

Nancy reported feeling a familiar urge to convince Ray to give it another try with his wife. She admitted that if this conversation had occurred in the past, she would have jumped all over him, shouted that it's never over, and blamed him for messing up—all to get him to take more responsibility.

Nancy said she had given it a second thought based on some class discussions about how blaming and accusations are huge obstacles between people's hearts, and she realized she didn't want to try forcing her son to return to his family using shaming and bullying.

Instead, she said, "Ray, I'm sorry that in the past I've blamed you for doing wrong and put a bunch of labels on you. I wish I had talked to you in a different way. Are you discouraged and feeling hopeless because you want peace at home? Maybe you're worried and wanting things with your wife to go easier? Do you hope to make it as a family and not end up divorced?"

Instead of answering her with his usual defensiveness, Ray broke down and cried. He began to tell his mother how much pain he was in and how much he loved his wife and baby. He was devastated. And he explicitly mentioned how relieved he was that Nancy was listening to him in this new way.

They continued for a few minutes, and although she got off the call feeling pleased with her new approach, Nancy didn't know what would happen between Ray and his wife because the situation had sounded pretty bleak. But when she spoke to him a couple days later, he announced that he had moved back home and he and his wife were starting to talk things out.

—MEGANWIND EOYANG, www.baynvc.org

---

*Our ability to offer empathy can allow us
to stay vulnerable, defuse potential violence,
hear the word* no *without taking it as a rejection,
revive a lifeless conversation, and even hear the
feelings and needs expressed through silence.*

—MARSHALL B. ROSENBERG, PhD

Empathy Cards During an Argument

When I met Daniel, he told me he had two emotions: angry and uncomfortable. It was only our first date, so I didn't push, but as an inner work junkie and very emotional person in general, I knew I would want to connect with him on a deeper emotional level.

At the beginning of our relationship I was learning about Nonviolent Communication. As I practiced this style of communicating, sometimes he would feel angry and say, "Why can't you just talk like a normal person? All you're doing is answering me in questions!"

In return, I accused him. "You're problem solving and I want empathy!"

I had heard of an empathy card game called GROK and I thought it might help us connect in a way that worked for both of us. In the game, one deck has Feelings cards (like Angry, Sad, and Happy) and the other deck has Needs (like Connection, Safety, and Health). He was reluctant to try it, but eventually he agreed to use the cards the next time we got into a disagreement.

That time came when Daniel told me he agreed to watch the dog he had shared with an ex-girlfriend while she was away. It was the same weekend we had planned to do a workshop together. When I realized he had no intention of changing his plans with his ex, I felt a lot of emotions, insecurities, and judgments. I also noticed that Daniel seemed defensive as we talked about it. We decided to use GROK cards to help us work it out.

He went first and placed some Feelings cards down—Torn, Overwhelmed, and Sad. He shared that his ex-girlfriend, Lily, was really concerned that she didn't have anyone to look after the dog. She wanted him to honor the commitment he had made when they got the dog together. He felt sad that he had forgotten about the workshop and was worried it would cause a rift between us. He also missed his dog and wanted to spend time with her.

I placed some Values cards down for him and asked, "Are integrity and support up for you right now? Wanting to honor your commitment to your dog and help out?"

He agreed and seemed more at ease. I continued, "Are you also wanting connection between you and your dog because you miss her?"

He replied, "Yes, and it seems like you get judgmental of me every time I spend time with her."

"So are you wanting a little more understanding about how important your dog is to you and the commitments you made?" I asked.

"Absolutely," he said. I saw his body relax.

When it was my turn to choose Feelings cards, I laid down the cards Disappointed, Worried, and Angry. I explained how disappointed I was that we weren't going to the workshop together because I was really looking forward to it. I also felt worried that he was choosing them over me, and I was angry that I thought that way.

Daniel responded, "It's hard to hear that you're disappointed in me."

"I'm not disappointed in you, I'm just disappointed. There's a difference," I said. He said he hadn't ever thought there was a difference between the two.

When he laid down the Values cards for me, he chose Security, Trust, and Intimacy.

He said, "It sounds like you were really looking forward to the closeness we would experience from going to this workshop together."

I nodded.

He continued, "Are you wanting to feel secure in our relationship and trust that when I make plans with you, I'll follow through?"

I noticed the pressure releasing in me as I heard his words, and I answered, "Yes, definitely."

It was such a turning point in our relationship, knowing that we could practice seeing things from the other person's point of view in a conflict. We felt so much closer after connecting in that way.

Another time I noticed he was upset about something. I asked him what was going on and he said, "I don't know! Just . . . get the cards!" I hid my smile as I went to get them. I was so happy he was willing to be brave and vulnerable to connect with me.

We no longer use the cards these days because we don't have to! Daniel has developed an awareness of his emotions and is happy to empathize with me when I'm struggling. I've grown in my ability to talk more normally when practicing empathy, and I'm better at focusing on listening instead of interrogating. We have developed a language we can use to connect with each other that is easy and deeply meaningful. We are so grateful!

—BECKA KELLEY

*Each of us carries some wisdom waiting
to be discovered at the center of our experience,
and everything we meet, if faced and held,
reveals a part of that wisdom.*

—MARK NEPO

Inner-Child Rescue

I was working in a class with a young woman who had difficulty with certain aspects of being a parent. When her young daughter felt angry, the woman became scared. She couldn't connect with her daughter or function well in those moments. She just froze.

I discovered the woman had grown up in a dangerous relationship with her mother that was not at all supportive of her well-being. Her mother had beaten her severely during bursts of anger, so badly that the police came.

We did what I call "time travel empathy," in which there's an internal dialogue or an inner "rescue" of sorts. It goes by different names, but it's a way of working with the parts of our brains that have remained alive to old experiences. When past incidents are unresolved, they stay awake in the memory and in our bodies too. This is a foundational starting point of post-traumatic stress.

I asked the young woman if she would be willing to go back in time and do a "rescue" for the little one in her who had been in such danger, and she agreed.

We traveled back in time. We froze time to make the environment safe. We froze her mother so that her mother was immobilized. We laid her mother down and put a sheet over her so that there was no longer any visual cue of her mother's anger or scariness in the room. Then we sat with this inner little girl and made empathy guesses for her.

We guessed that she felt really scared, more than anything else. And we wondered if she needed to know she was being seen, that she existed, and that her needs mattered. We touched on her feelings of frozenness, terror, overwhelm, physical pain, and helplessness.

As we did this, the woman recognized how much her inner child needed to be protected, and that no one expects their own mother to be a source of pain and terror.

I asked her to stay tuned in to this image of her own body as a little girl. As we continued making guesses about her needs and feelings, the little girl uncurled from a fetal position and slowly stood up. The woman who was receiving empathy "watched" the unfolding and said, "Oh my goodness, she's so strong!"

I asked if she wanted to bring back her earlier self to the present time. Of course, she had already survived all those years and did not need to live through them again. The little girl trapped in her memory was simply that—trapped. She was caught in the past because it was hard, and she was unaccompanied there. We invited this little one to come back to the present, and found she was willing to do so. She slipped through time and space back to the here-and-now. The woman was so relieved to have her own little one back with her.

"Now think about your daughter's face when she's angry. How does is it feel?" I asked.

"Oh, she's just a little girl. She looks like me and she looks like her dad. She doesn't just look like her grandma anymore. Now I wonder what she's so angry about."

It seemed clear that after traveling through time to connect with her inner child, this woman had a very different sense of her own child's anger. About a month later, I checked in to find out if her new experience was stable.

She said, "Yes! I'm not frightened of my daughter when she gets upset anymore!"

I think this speaks to the power of empathy to change lives and support people's well-being on so many levels.

—SARAH PEYTON, www.yourresonantself.com

We need empathy to give empathy.

—MARSHALL B. ROSENBERG, PhD

Blueberry Meltdown

As I was working in my office one day, I heard my three-year-old daughter screaming. My home office was in a tiny bedroom with a thin door, so I could hear everything. She was in the dining room having a tremendous tantrum, complete with yelling and kicking. I gave it a little time, but it just kept going and going. I knew my wife was with her, but the situation wasn't improving.

I tried to focus and stay in the concentrated space I was in, but I was distracted and irritated by the yelling.

So I charged out of my office, thinking, *I need her to shut up! I need quiet!*

I got within a few feet of my daughter as I charged into the room. I wanted to say something like *What is wrong with you? Keep it down!* But as I got closer, something clicked. I stopped, took a deep breath, and turned my attention inward.

In that pause, I repeated internally, *I need her to shut up.* But then I asked myself, *If I get her to be quiet, what will I have? What will that give me? What's really going on is that I need a different level of support, and more quiet time would really help that.*

As soon as I got connected with my feelings and my needs, I felt something shift!

I was no longer on a warpath to get my child to shut up. I had become connected with myself and felt a change.

I found I was able to be present with her and get curious. I said, "What happened? What's going on?"

Well, it turned out that Mom had given her a bowl of blueberries with milk, and several blueberries had fallen out of the bowl and onto the floor. In her three-year-old mind, this had shattered the *perfection* of this bowl of blueberries.

I asked her, "If I get you three more blueberries, will that help?"

"Yeah!" she said.

I got her three more blueberries and her crying stopped, the tantrum stopped, and all the kicking stopped.

It wasn't because I connected with my need for quiet that did the trick. It was about me seeking connection with my daughter to find out what we could do that would meet both of our needs.

Self-empathy helps me make that kind of shift. If I didn't have self-empathy skills, I might have a very different connection with my children. They might see me as an irritable ogre. Instead, I'm willing to self-connect, slow down, and think, *What's going on? If there's a strategy here, let's find it.*

That's the difference. That's the kind of easy shift I can make using self-empathy. And those little shifts make a big difference in my relationships.

—ALAN SEID, www.cascadiaworkshops.com

---

*The gentle and sensitive companionship
offered by an empathic person . . . provides
illumination and healing. In such situations
deep understanding is, I believe, the most
precious gift one can give to another.*

—CARL ROGERS

Different Ways of
Showing Love for Our Baby

When my wife and I bought our house, I was pregnant, so we were under a time constraint to get things done before the baby came. We agreed to focus on certain priorities, knowing we wouldn't have time to complete everything. We knew, for instance, that we'd need to finish the bathroom before we had a home birth.

My wife was a perfectionist who paid attention to details like no one I'd ever met. She also had woodworking skills, so she took charge of most of the house projects. As she worked on getting the cabinets in, she sent me off to do other tasks, and I was supposed to come back right away to help with the next step. This system worked most of the time, but as we both felt the pressure of the ticking clock, we became annoyed with each other.

"Would you go measure this?" she asked. "It's going right here, so measure it."

A few minutes later, I replied, "It's about twelve and a half inches."

"No, I need to know what it is to the sixty-fourth of an inch. That's what measuring is."

"Okay. It's twelve and a half."

She was irritated with my sloppy measuring, which made sense because I was a sloppy measurer. I didn't even know that kind of marking on a tape measure existed. I'd never counted the sixty-fourths before.

She was so frustrated. "You know, I have to do this right."

"EMPATHY NOTS"
Example

EDUCATING

"Worrying doesn't help."
"Every story has two sides."

"It's underneath, so nobody will see it anyway!" I replied.

That sent her into fits of fire spitting and the like. After we decided I should stay away from the tasks involving measuring, I began to understand what her precision was really about.

"Is it that you want this bathroom to be beautiful and functional and for all of the pieces to fit together nicely?"

"Yes, yes!" she said. "You need to measure to the sixty-fourth of an inch!"

The story in my head that she was too picky and controlling suddenly gave way.

"So you want this to be beautiful. You want us to live in this house for a very long time, and you want all of the pieces to fit together."

She breathed and it felt like there was an exhalation in the space itself. The air in the room had felt electrically charged and mean before, but it softened immediately. We smiled at each other and at our wonderful new home.

—KRISTIN MASTERS, www.nvcsantacruz.org

---

*The objective of NVC is not to change people
and their behavior in order to get our way;
it is to establish relationships based on
honesty and empathy that will eventually
fulfill everyone's needs.*

—MARSHALL B. ROSENBERG, PhD

Bedroom Lies

Long after our breakup, my ex-boyfriend and I found ourselves flirting our way down a familiar romantic path—toward his bedroom. I knew we'd be having sex soon and I was enjoying the fling, feeling comfortable and sparky at the same time.

As Gary and I undressed each other, fully turned on, I realized that some of the agreements we had in the past may not still be in effect. While we were dating, we had a clear idea of when it was okay to have sex with other partners, when it wasn't, and how we'd handle sexual safety in the context of intimacy. We often didn't use condoms together, but the expectation was that we would let the other person know if or when a new sexy friend entered the picture, at which point we'd discuss and reexamine things. This worked for us the entire time we were dating.

Quite some time had passed since Gary and I had been intimate, and I hadn't been with anyone since him. But I knew how much he liked *not* using condoms, so I thought I'd check in. If he'd had sex with anyone else since then, I was clear I'd want him to rubber up.

"Hey, we should talk about protection. Unless you haven't been with anybody since the last time we had sex. Have you?"

I'd like to say I paused long enough to give him space to think, but I was already pulling him back in as he shook his head no, and on we went. The whole conversation was over in seconds.

After we had a fantastic, steamy reunion, Gary hung his head and said, "Look. This is hard to say for a few reasons. When I said I hadn't slept with another woman, I lied. I have."

Stunned, I sat there. It took me a moment to register his words. He wanted to have unprotected sex, so he told me a lie. He knew exactly what was important to me, but it didn't matter. Selfishness. Violation. Breach of consent. It was almost unfathomable because I had so much trust in him. Trust had never been our issue.

I had no words, I was so shocked.

He stammered through my silence: "And . . . I'm not even sure what else to say, because I know how you see this. But there it is. I'm really sorry."

I could barely process all my thoughts, but I decided to just repeat back his words.

"So. You're telling me that when I asked about your activity and protection earlier, you lied. And now you want me to know. Is that what I'm hearing right now?"

He nodded, looking guilty. *Good!*

I continued. "I'm guessing, in the moment when I asked, you were really in the flow of things and wanted to stay in it."

It didn't seem possible, but his shoulders and face dropped even lower as he nodded yes, feebly. *Good!*

"You're feeling guilty now? But in that moment, for you it was about continuity and pleasure . . . and reveling in how good it felt to be back together. Yes?"

"Exactly," Gary muttered. "But now as I look at you and the anger on your face, all I can do is . . . judge myself. I was being immature and selfish. I just did what I wanted to do. It's nice hearing you try to understand, but I almost can't let you let me off the hook."

I laughed bitterly. "Trust me, you're so not off the hook. I have those same thoughts about you running in loops. It's no excuse, but I'm reaching for the part of me that gets what it's like to feel so turned on that I don't want to be interrupted for anything. But I'm an adult, for God's sake, and I care about consent. When I think about that . . . !"

I stopped. I couldn't finish my sentence.

"I know. I'm really sorry. *Really* sorry," he said.

"Listen, I hear you. And I know how much you care about integrity, so I get that you're sorry after the fact. But I'm not really feeling myself softening. I'm furious. I can't imagine how it was okay in your mind to lie to me like that."

"Well, I can explain a little, even though it might make things worse. I can tell you how I justified it. But I know it doesn't excuse things!" he said with a low voice, cringing.

I braced myself.

"The person I slept with . . . well, it was Diane. She's someone you've known about, someone we've agreed about before. And I told myself you wouldn't care, since it hadn't mattered in the past."

A flash of heat went through my chest. Empathy begone!

"It doesn't matter what I decided about Diane in the past! I might've made the same decision, or I might not have. That's up to me! I don't know what Diane's been up to sexually since we last talked about it, however long ago. I'd have some questions!"

"I know." He slumped over.

I continued, shaking my head in dismay. "I didn't get a chance to choose! You chose for me without even telling me!"

"I know. I did. I can see how it affects you, and I can see how things have turned a corner in our time together today. I really wish I'd done it differently."

"Listen," I said. "I need to take a moment to myself. I appreciate everything you're saying, and I'm sure these waves running through me will continue to do their thing. I just don't know how long it'll take before I'm ready to keep talking about this. Not to mention that we need to get into a whole other conversation about Diane and what you two did together. I mean, now I have to get tested. Ugh!"

He nodded.

"I can't tell, at least not right now, if I'll need anything from you to repair this or not."

"That makes sense," he said.

"I want you to know I can see you're sad," I said, my voice thawing a bit. "But it will take some time. I don't know how long."

"Okay, totally fine," he said, nodding. "You want a bit of space from this. Does dinner sound good? Then we can see if there's more to say after that. And if you need even more time, I get it."

"Okay. Food would be good," I replied.

We had a productive conversation that evening and again several days later. I was glad things hadn't gone too sideways between us—it made it easier to work through the pain of such a boundary breach.

—ANONYMOUS

> *I have since identified a specific approach to communicating—both speaking and listening— that leads us to give from the heart, connecting us with ourselves and with each other in a way that allows our natural compassion to flourish. I call this approach Nonviolent Communication.*
>
> —MARSHALL B. ROSENBERG, PhD

Overwhelmed Granny

My youngest granddaughters spent a lot of time with me when they were young. There were enjoyable moments and challenging ones too. When they were about eight and ten years old, they played well together overall, but from time to time, things would devolve.

It usually began with Samantha, the younger one, calling out, "Granny, Jessica's being mean to me!"

These few simple words often inspired Jessica to take it up a notch or two.

As soon as I heard this plaintive tone of Sam's, I felt overwhelmed and discouraged. *Oh no, here we go again!* I thought. The timing of this exchange usually happened when I was tired and not feeling resourceful. Then I would pray for their parents to arrive to take them home.

After they went home, I felt relief that they were out of my hair, but the internal self-blaming and criticism began. *I'm a terrible grandmother. Grandparents aren't supposed to get like this. It's supposed to be all dreamy and wonderful. They're my grandchildren! I'm supposed to love them unconditionally and never feel irritated or impatient! Nothing like this happens for any other grandmothers— only me.*

One day, after I'd attended a communication workshop, something different happened. As the girls began to bicker, it occurred to me to try listening to them as I'd heard about in the workshop. I took a breath, felt that familiar hopelessness, and noticed that I wanted to shout, *Oh for heaven's sake, stop it. Why don't you get along?*

But in that moment, I didn't. Instead, I took some deep breaths and said something like, "Gosh, are you feeling kind of sad, Samantha?"

Suddenly, it was a different world in my house.

I took another breath and reflected with her. "What was it that happened?"

We investigated together about why they were on each other's cases. And I felt resourceful, at least briefly. It was enough to get me through the moment.

I was amazed to see that I had a different option than the usual *Oh good grief, they're fighting again. I wish their parents would hurry up and get here.*

I'm glad I can laugh about it now. It took me a while to realize that it was okay to feel irritated and to wish they'd stop fighting. I was doing the best I could. It was also nice to learn I could do things differently, which helped me connect with my granddaughters more easily on those harder days.

—ANNE WALTON, www.chooseconnection.com

> *When you show deep empathy toward others,*
> *their defensive energy goes down, and positive*
> *energy replaces it. That's when you can get*
> *more creative in solving problems.*

—STEPHEN COVEY

Kitty Empathy

Several months earlier, I passed by a van full of cats from the American Society for the Prevention of Cruelty to Animals. I went over to take a look and saw a cat called Caiden. I love Irish names, so he caught my attention. I already had two cats at home and wasn't looking for a third, but I couldn't resist Caiden. He was so affectionate, such a lover boy, sticking to me like Velcro. He was like a baby wanting to be held. I couldn't leave him in the van, so Caiden came home with me.

My housemate was surprised and so were my other cats. The ASPCA told me what to do when introducing new cats and I followed all the steps. I kept him in my bedroom and the cats smelled each other under the door. Everything seemed fine.

One day, though, Caiden clearly got tired of being shut away in one room. He escaped and all hell broke loose. I could never have guessed that this warm, sweet, affectionate, and doting little guy could show such aggression toward other cats. He made a beeline for my cat Seamus and attacked him. Seamus yowled in terror. I had to separate him from this giant ball of fur. It was horrifying.

I was alarmed and shouted at Caiden, "Stop it! Stop it!

Leave him alone!" I felt so sad and concerned for Seamus. It was horrifying to watch how he hunted Seamus down. The other cat, Addy, hid in the closet and tried to stay out of trouble!

For eight weeks, the fighting continued, even though I tried to keep them separated. When I let them outside, thinking it would give them some space, Caiden tracked Seamus down and I could hear the howling and screaming of another fight. I've grown up with cats, and I had never seen anything like it. It went on for weeks.

I called the animal clinic when these troubles started and described the fighting to the pet behavioral psychologist. Her response was pretty discouraging.

She said, "Hmm, I hate to tell you this, but I think you should find another home for Caiden. I don't think it will work in the long term. The behavior you're describing—attacking other cats—is kind of extreme. Maybe Caiden needs to be a solo cat."

So I began looking for a new home for Caiden, even though I was sad about it. I didn't want to give him up! Each time the cats got into a fight, I ran over to stop it. I was determined.

My housemate said, "Dian, I think you're actually making it worse because you get so scared when they're fighting. You get stressed and start shouting at them!"

It made sense. I hadn't thought about it before, but it's normal for fear to turn up as aggression. I wondered if my fear was ramping up the aggressive energy between the cats, because I knew they were both scared to begin with.

This realization gave me new compassion for Caiden. I had been confused about how loving he was with me, but how vicious he was with other cats. It all made sense now. He wanted love so badly that he felt threatened and insecure around the other cats. Of course he felt afraid! He was in a new environment and the other cats were there first.

I completely changed my strategy. I picked up Caiden and gave him lots of love before Seamus came in. I talked to him: "I just want you to know, I'm so glad you're here. I really like your company. I think you'll really like Seamus because he enjoys being with other cats."

At first Seamus was afraid to come into the house when he saw this monster on my lap. He entered tentatively, while keeping his eye on us. Caiden was antsy, but I kept petting and using a soothing voice, trying to imagine how they both wanted some calmness and peace. And soon, they both relaxed.

After eight weeks of fighting and worrying that I'd have to find another home for Caiden, things settled. The whole situation changed. Now they groom each other daily, sleep in the same bed, play together, and even choose to eat from the same bowl. When I first saw their aggressive behavior together, I never imagined they would eventually groom each other. At most, I hoped they might tolerate each other, like a cold war. Instead, the connection between them completely transformed. I wonder what the pet expert would say if she knew how things changed! It's really an empathy miracle!

—DIAN KILLIAN, www.workcollaboratively.com

*Only after all needs have been mutually heard, do
we progress to the solutions stage: making doable
requests using positive, action language.*

—MARSHALL B. ROSENBERG, PhD

When Your Kid Hates School

Last year, our family took on a "homeschooled-girl-tries-out-school-and-hates-it" experiment. My eleven-year-old daughter wanted to go to school, but after a few weeks she suddenly changed her mind. I drove her to school one morning and she refused to go.

Her dad and I were eager for her to stick it out for a while. With her at school, I could work more hours and have more financial sustainability. So when she changed her mind on the way to school that day, I felt thrown off.

We sat down outside the building and I asked, "Sweetie, what's going on?"

"I don't feel like it," she replied. She said she *might* be getting sick.

I told her that people who go to school often don't feel like it. And, I went on, they even go when they are tired or have a slight cold.

"Honey," I said. "Daddy really wants you to go! I want you to! What don't you enjoy about it? Is it your teacher? The kids?"

She exploded. "Mom! I just want empathy!"

I sat in silence, stunned. Time stopped for me. The universe waited.

I began to cry.

You see, around the time my baby girl turned four years old, I began studying the key principles of connection. I put a lot of attention—for years—on the way I wanted to be with others in my life, and how I wanted to show up for my family.

I focused hours of energy learning about how to be with people in full presence, by listening to their experience, intuitively guessing their deepest needs, and sharing my most authentic truth. These were all values I'd hoped to pass on to my children: the importance of compassion, the power of empathy, and the impact of giving and receiving it.

So I wasn't crying because I had failed to offer her empathy. I had compassion for myself for that. And I wasn't crying because she was angry with me.

I had tears in my eyes because I was overwhelmed by the most profound sense that I'd attained the thing I'd most wanted to accomplish as a parent. I had taught my child to *expect empathy*. And to ask for it when it wasn't happening. To me, this was huge.

I wiped my tears away, took a breath, and shifted gears.

At that point, I didn't care about anything else in the world. I said, "You're so sad and just want me to listen?"

She nodded. I asked if she was feeling tired and wanting understanding. I asked if she just wanted to rest and have a choice about school.

She ended up deciding, after a few minutes, to go to class that day. And she did so with willingness. I suppose she just needed a moment to be heard. Those moments outside the school gave me hope for the world. If every child could experience empathy and collaboration, and not simply be told what to do every time an adult is in a rush, the world could be a very different place.

—CEDAR ROSE SELENITE

Ask before offering advice or reassurance.

—MARSHALL B. ROSENBERG, PhD

A Friend's Unsolicited Advice About My Ex

I was going through an extremely challenging and painful divorce process. My sense of fairness, financial security, and even sharing a common worldview with my soon-to-be ex-wife were challenged in the biggest ways possible.

One incredibly stressful issue was my living situation. My ex still lived in the house I had purchased before we got married, and she wouldn't leave or offer any money for rent. I needed to get renters into the house because I was running out of money to pay the monthly mortgage. I was especially frustrated because she had plenty of assets and resources to get her own place.

My best friend offered his advice about the whole situation. "Why don't you just move back into the house, since it's yours? That will make her uncomfortable and she'll get out."

I ignored his advice, but when we spoke on the phone a short time later, he brought it up again.

He said, "Let's move you into your house today, with her still in it. Seriously. I think that facing the pain and not avoiding what needs to be done is good relationship advice and life wisdom."

"No, I'm not moving in today, but thanks for reminding me of that possibility. I'll consider it and see if there are any legal implications."

"Listen," he replied, "she's not uncomfortable enough! She'll leave if you make her uncomfortable. Living in your house is being right in the fire. Will there be conflict? Yes, but it's better than going through lawyers. You'll be dealing with things directly. So make love with another woman in your house, where your ex will have to hear it! Please don't rule these ideas out. You'll save lots of money by using your wits."

"Look," I said, "I'm not averse to the possibility of moving in. I also want to make sure I don't hurt my case or get a restraining order against me. I need to figure out what's involved. There are also psychological challenges for me in that scenario. I don't know if I have it in me to face that much conflict and dissonance."

"Well, I think it's a flipping great idea. It's the perfect idea. Hard to imagine a restraining order could apply. You aren't harassing her. You're just moving back in."

"I discussed this scenario with someone, and I recall that 'automatic' restraining orders could be put in place under certain circumstances when couples separate. I need to check it out."

"She needs to be made uncomfortable. How about a hot tub date with another woman at two in the morning? Find out. But do it. She needs this. And it will be good for you!"

"Okay. Enough." I said. "I don't want any more advice on this. I understand your position."

"If you don't do something, my respect for you will waver," he countered.

"Super unsupportive."

"Not true! The truth is *you* created this. Only *you* can go into that lair and slay that dragon, unarmed with lawyers. You're being chickenshit."

I was incredulous, but apparently so was he.

"I'm done," he said. "I'm going to work to help folks deal with real serious problems now . . . without lawyers! Done! Goodbye."

I sighed, took a breath, and said, "I'm working so damn hard on this divorce thing. I'm doing everything I know how, using my best intelligence. Hearing from my dear friend that his respect for me will waver if I don't act as he sees fit is not what I need right now. And then you follow up by calling me chickenshit? I feel hurt, sad, and angry about that."

He responded, "Hey, listen. Whatever you choose to do."

With that, the conversation was over. I spent the next hour using all the self-connection tools I could think of to navigate my intense feelings and thoughts. I decided to reach out to him to see how I could resolve this interaction.

"Hey," I said when I called him back. "I did a little work around our conflict, and I'm guessing it's frustrating for you to witness the bullshit that my ex is putting me through and getting away with. I imagine that's what motivated some of your strong opinions and statements."

I felt a calmness come between us immediately as he said, "Very insightful. That's exactly it. By the way, beautiful communication skills."

"Thanks. To be honest, I'm kind of impressed myself. It would have been easy to stay in reaction, but using what I've learned about empathy, I thought to consider what needs of yours might be underneath all of this. That helped me interpret what you were saying as coming from a core desire for fairness, justice, and true concern for your friend."

"Yes, exactly! I'm feeling a heightened sense of injustice *for* you. You are my closest friend and what she's trying to pull off seems so mean. I apologize for taking it too far. I'm sorry. I'm here to support you in whatever way I can."

And from there, we were able to get back on track and get on with our day.

—ANONYMOUS

*Self-forgiveness: connecting with the need
we were trying to meet when we took
the action that we now regret.*

—MARSHALL B. ROSENBERG, PhD

Time-Out!

My six-year-old grandson, Anton, went with me to the science museum and was beside himself with excitement. When we arrived, he played on the red ropes at the entrance. Then he took off, running into the crowd, dodging people, and disappearing. When I saw him again, he was swinging on the red ropes while people tried to move through the line, and I said, sharply, "Anton, get over here right now!"

He was having so much fun on the rope, but he instantly crumpled at the sound of my voice. He came over with his head down so low.

I said, "I need a time-out here."

"Okay," he replied, looking around to see where he might sit.

I smiled wryly and exclaimed, "Not for you, for me!"

He looked at me with big eyes. "What?"

"I don't like the way I just talked to you," I replied. "I don't want to talk to anyone that way, especially not my beloved grandson. So I'm giving myself a time-out to think it over."

He was truly stupefied, looking at me in wonder while I sat against the wall right there in the line. He sat as close to me as he possibly could, curled up and leaning on my leg. We sat that way for several minutes, quietly.

"Well, that was about five minutes," I said. "I think I learned my lesson because I've been thinking it over."

He continued looking at me with bewilderment, so I said, "Do *you* think I learned my lesson?"

He nodded his head solemnly. "Yes."

"Then let's go have fun here at the science center!" And we went on our way.

Some people might think I was right to scold him when he was running around, but I realized he was just being a kid. I wanted to explain to him a little more about my perspective, so later that morning I did.

"Look," I said, "I want to tell you why I was upset earlier."

He seemed totally willing to hear it.

"I was scared when I didn't know where you were. Then when I saw you pulling on the ropes, I was worried the posts might fall over and hurt someone."

He got it. He nodded, and I knew we had connected completely differently than if I'd tried to convey the same thing earlier in a sharp, intense way.

—MAIR ALIGHT, www.mairalight.com

---

*By maintaining our attention on what's
going on within others, we offer them a chance
to fully explore and express their interior selves.
We would stem this flow if we were to shift
attention too quickly either to their request
or to our own desire to express ourselves.*

—MARSHALL B. ROSENBERG, PhD

Teenage Gratitude

My partner had photographed our teenage daughter receiving the winner's trophy at a sporting event. Thinking she would be delighted, he enlarged the photo, framed it, and placed it on a table in our entry.

I was relieved he wasn't home when she first saw it. She took one look at the photo and exclaimed, "Who took that photo?! It's crap!"

I couldn't believe it! *How ungrateful! How selfish can she be? Doesn't she realize the love that went into creating this gift?* All kinds of thoughts flashed through my mind. I wondered what kind of mother I was to bring up such a selfish child.

Luckily, I had attended an introductory communication workshop the night before where the facilitator said that "all violence is a tragic expression of unmet needs." I was certainly experiencing her words as violent, but what needs were underlying them? I remembered hearing that one important need, especially for teenagers, is choice.

I also remembered that, no matter what she said, her outburst was *not about me*. So I followed the instructions from the workshop and took a deep breath. And then a second one. I used that time to get in touch with my own need for recognition of my husband's love in putting the picture together.

A bit tentatively, I asked my daughter, "Would you like to choose the pictures of you that are displayed?"

"Yes!" she exclaimed. "Dad should have asked me first. It's a stupid picture!"

Taking another breath, I decided to stay with the same theme of choice, which was all I could think of.

"So I guess you're really frustrated and having choice is important to you?" I asked.

I heard her mumble, "Uh-huh." Apparently, I was on track.

She looked down, her shoulders sagging. Still feeling confused and unsure of the next best step, I asked if it would be okay to put the photo in her dad's office. She agreed.

When I returned, I discovered my daughter with her head in her arms, sobbing. Between sobs, she looked up at me and said, "It's not about the picture. It's about . . ."

And she began to tell me about a work experience that day that was very painful for her. I listened quietly, feeling immense gratitude for the few prompts I'd learned that made space for this moment.

I was so glad I hadn't expressed my earlier thoughts about her being ungrateful and selfish when she was already feeling so raw and tender.

Because I looked for something behind the words I initially found so challenging, I had a treasured opportunity to support her and to deepen the connection between us. That connection is precious. Especially with a teenager!

After my daughter recovered, she asked, "Where did you put the picture?"

I told her it was in her dad's office.

"Oh," she replied. "Let's put it back in the entry . . . it's really okay."

The photo has been proudly displayed there, front and center, ever since.

—PENNY WASSMAN, www.pennywassman.ca

---

*We stay with empathy and allow others
the opportunity to fully express themselves
before we turn our attention to solutions
or requests for relief.*

—MARSHALL B. ROSENBERG, PhD

Saying No, Holding Us Both

I have struggled with saying no since childhood. As a people-pleaser (or codependent), I've long believed that the well-being of others depends on me fulfilling their wants and needs, often to the point of ignoring my own. Learning about and practicing Nonviolent Communication has been life-changing. I have learned to distinguish between my thoughts and feelings and to honor my needs without disrespecting others.

While dabbling in online dating for the past year, I've had some new opportunities to say no. As someone who came of age in the 1980s, it took several months to warm up to communicating through texts and emails. Once I decided to go on a few dates, I quickly became overwhelmed by the challenge of engaging with strangers who were looking to get their desires fulfilled.

My first impulse was to use the "ghosting" method of ceasing all communications with certain men I felt uncomfortable with. But I also wanted to grow, and I knew that shying away from edgy conversations would not help me stretch my comfort zone. I wanted to figure out how to prioritize my needs while respecting those who reached out to me.

I decided to practice with Lance who I felt especially noncommittal about. We'd only been on one date when he disappeared for some time and then suddenly reappeared, wanting urgently to get together again. I said I wasn't interested, but he accused me of giving up without giving him a full chance.

I tuned into my thoughts. I remember feeling relieved when I hadn't heard back from Lance after our first date. He wanted to come over to my place before we had even met, which was a red flag for me. I also noticed that his failure to acknowledge his disappearance really bothered me.

I pushed through multiple levels of discomfort to continue communicating with Lance until I felt I had responded thoughtfully but honestly to his requests to reconnect. My biggest source of angst came from the fear of attack or criticism if I expressed wants that differed from his (or anyone else's for that matter). I needed courage to confront this fear and empowerment to unapologetically voice my true desires.

I decided to let Lance know that I didn't want to spend more time together, but I wanted to tell him in a way I thought was kind and candid.

So when he said, "I'd really like to see you again," I reflected that back and then told him I wasn't interested in that.

I said, "Do you remember when I told you that my father was ill a while back? Well, he passed, and I'm really not in a state of mind to start a new relationship."

"But I really like you," he insisted. "Will you take some more time to think about it?" He wanted me to explain my needs on a deeper level and how I thought they clashed with his.

I said, "Frankly, no. I think we want two different things. You seem to be mainly interested in sex. I'd like to get to know someone better before deciding if or when to have sex. There's nothing wrong with that; we just want different things."

I had no idea how Lance would react to my repeated refusals, but he said, "Okay. Thank you for explaining. I'm here if you ever decide to change your mind."

I felt moved by his respect and appreciation. Explaining to him why I was staying firm in my decision, rooted in empathy for both of us, made all the difference. Saying no had never felt so empowering and thoughtful.

—MARY ROAF

*To listen is to continually give up all expectation
and to give our attention, completely and freshly,
to what is before us, not really knowing what
we will hear or what that will mean.*

—MARK NEPO

Don't Just Do Something

One evening, I was incredibly frustrated with my husband. We were expecting company to arrive any minute, but instead of cleaning up his clutter, he was sitting in his chair.

I launched into a lecture about responsibility, and I could almost see him retreating into himself as I berated him about being insensitive. It was the beginning of a familiar communication logjam, and I realized my menacing thoughts were about to take over. Minutes before, I had been excited about having a fun evening with friends, but now everything seemed tied up.

I sighed. I felt hopeless as I thought about where this argument was headed. Yet I was suddenly aware of my distress in a new way.

As I took a brief pause from what I was saying, I noticed the tightness in my head and chest, my quick heartbeat, and my shallow breath. I realized I had probably been oblivious to these signs in the past. As I thought about this, my mind flashed back to a workshop I'd attended recently in which Marshall Rosenberg shared his twist on the familiar saying, "Don't just stand there, do something."

"Don't just do something . . .," Marshall said, lingering for dramatic effect, " . . . stand there!" It had caught my attention, and I made a note of it.

As I glanced at the clock, in anticipation of the doorbell ringing, I felt some clarity. I knew I didn't want another emotionally draining experience that led to the same old logjam between me and my husband.

Yet I didn't know what else to do. Dumbfounded about how to make a shift, I just stood there, waiting for an idea of what to say next. *Okay, Marshall. I'm just standing here instead of doing something, so now what? If you talked about what came next, I don't remember it.*

I continued to stand still, looking at my husband—far longer than was familiar or comfortable. Gradually, the tightness in my chest melted away. My breathing deepened. I felt cooler.

Minutes passed, and in this unfamiliar state of calm, I held at bay the desire to do something—anything.

Standing there, not lecturing or railing at him, I felt closer to my husband and recalled something else from the workshop: "Skip the explanations and lectures; just ask for what you want."

"Would you please pick up your things now?" I ventured.

"Sure," my husband answered.

—VICTORIA KINDLE HODSON, www.thenofaultzone.com

Attention is the rarest and purest form of generosity.

—SIMONE WEIL

Increasing Intimacy With One Question

In my twenties, I had one particular relationship in which I became an expert at hiding pain. Conversations with my boyfriend often shifted away from my feelings and instead focused on his sadness, confusion, or defensiveness, especially if my distress had anything to do with him. I learned to cry silently and without obvious body movement. Even while cuddling, with my back to him and his forearm cradling my head, I hid my tears along with any sorrow, confusion, or pain.

I deemed myself the silent sob master. These were my mantras in these moments: *Do not let tears spill, Breathe slowly, Do not gasp for air in between silent sobs*, and *This too shall pass.*

What a difference two decades can make. Recently, I fractured three ribs. While navigating an enormous amount of discomfort and immobility, I was lucky to be seeing a man who knew how to ask about and stay with my feelings.

A week after being injured, we lay together on my calico bedspread from India as he gently caressed my arm. Like a South Asian version of Klimt's *The Kiss*, we stayed there for some time talking and making jokes, trying not to agitate my constant hum of pain with any movement or deep laughter.

Enjoying the ebb and flow of conversation and the spaces of

perfect and serene silence, I appreciated this pause from the chaos of injury, pain, and family. Tears began to flow. And I calmly allowed myself to be seen, not that I could have moved to hide even if I tried.

New lovers can be especially nervous around tears and the possible meaning of each tear (unpredictable emotions, accusations, or problems), but this man expressed curiosity. Gently and with care, he asked, "Okay . . . what's going on?"

I was a little unclear myself and not used to being asked. I looked within and realized they were tears of relief. The previous week had been so challenging. In that moment, I was reveling in the sweetness of his unannounced visit, the gifts of flowers and chocolates he'd brought, and his present embrace. He was unsuspectingly winning my heart.

Embarrassed, I said, "Nothing."

He stuck with me. "Tears are always about something."

There was something about the safety and Klimt-like entanglement of our embrace that helped me relax further into his strong arms, as he kept showing up and inquiring. So I said what I was most sure about. "It's been a really hard week with my family here. All that family disconnection, my fractured ribs, the pain . . ." I reflected, "and it's simply so sweet to be held by you."

When I'm vulnerable, each gesture of holding and each curious question calms my system a little more. I become more able to receive his nourishing compassion. He relaxed into the clarity that my tears were an emotional release, not the kind that are angry or sad. He hadn't done anything but love me in just the right way.

I nuzzled my face into his neck as he cooed a soft "aww," and we nestled further into each other, the moment, and our sweet connection in the silence beyond our quiet breathing.

My mantra these days is that simply noticing, holding, and asking . . . can be enough.

—SHEILA MENEZES, www.compassionatereturn.com

*The most important thing in communication
is hearing what isn't said.*

—PETER DRUCKER

Bike-Riding Mishap

On a visit with my daughter when she was in college, we decided to try out a funky bicycle built for two that a friend had given her. We weren't even sure if we could ride it, but it looked like fun.

She was having a grumpy morning, but we got on the bike—her in front, me in back—and off we rode. Within a few minutes, we were moving along quickly.

Soon there was a situation where my instincts simultaneously prompted me to yell, "Brake!" and to backpedal in an attempt to slow the bike down.

It didn't work.

Instead of braking, the chain jumped off the sprockets and we came to an abrupt and scary stop in a grassy area. We were safe, but my daughter was livid.

"What were you thinking?" she shouted angrily and continued ranting.

This was some time ago, but I still remember a calmness coming over me, a feeling of dropping into my body. I knew her anger resulted from the shock and fear of the unexpected, lurching stop. But she was quite upset and seemed to think it was all my fault. The ride looked like it might be ruined as she stopped yelling and stomped away.

I stayed with the calmness in my body, feeling silent empathy for her. Then I said something like, "You're upset and not sure you feel like riding more?"

She nodded, almost imperceptibly.

I continued, "That was surprising and pretty scary!"

"EMPATHY NOTS"
Example

EVALUATING

"Sounds like he has issues."
"She obviously doesn't care."

I waited another moment, then owned my part by acknowledging that what I did had, in fact, landed us in the grass. I invited her to help me get the chain back on, so we could continue to ride.

She walked over to me and the bike, crouched down, and we worked together to put the chain back on. Within a few minutes, we were ready to continue the ride. What could've been a disastrous interaction turned into one of repair and reconnection.

—JEAN MORRISON, www.nvcsantacruz.org

*Time and again, I have witnessed people
transcend the paralyzing effects of psychological
pain when they have sufficient contact with
someone who can hear them empathically.*

—MARSHALL B. ROSENBERG, PhD

The Little Lamb

It was a Saturday evening when I heard the kids' excited voices as they were approaching the house and calling me.

"Aya! Ayaaa!"

"What? What?" I asked as I rushed to the door.

I saw Michael, my son, standing on the stairs with a little lamb in his hands.

"What is this?!" I exclaimed.

"It's a little lamb," he said with sadness in his voice. "She was born yesterday, and her mother doesn't let her near. She is very weak. She may die."

Michael came in with the tiny lamb, followed by his brother Dan-Dan and his friends Deon and Dana.

Before I had a chance to say anything, they laid her down on their Spider-Man blanket and covered her with an old rug.

The baby lamb didn't look so good. She couldn't stand on her feet and her eyes gazed at one imaginary point.

"We took her to Rebeca," said my husband, Shahar, as he came through the door. "She said these things happen from time to time. We found her too late and there isn't much chance that she will survive because she needs her mother's milk to strengthen her immune system. But we can try to give her some cow milk from a bottle."

And then he added, "I need to go soon. Will you take care of it?"

To my untrained ears, it didn't sound like I had any choice . . . but that is a topic for another time. As I sat for a bit with the four kids and, apparently, a dying lamb in the house, I noticed how much I wanted her to live. My heart was full of compassion for the fragile creature that had just landed in my life. I realized I was willing to do whatever I could to help her survive. And I was not the only one.

Forty-year-old me, eight-year-old Michael, six-year-old Deon, five-year-old Dan-Dan, and little three-year-old Dana all had the same response. We felt unconditional love for the helpless, vulnerable baby animal.

As Dan-Dan put it, "Aya, I can't stop thinking about the lamb, and I don't know why."

"I can understand that, Dan-Dan," I said, "because I'm feeling the same as you. I am having frequent thoughts about her too. I believe it is in our human nature to feel compassion when we are facing life in its vulnerability. We humans care. This is how we are."

Michael seemed to appoint himself the person in charge and began feeding her with a bottle. But the lamb was too weak to suck from it.

"She will live, right, Aya?" he implored. "She has to live!" he said, desperate for reassurance.

"We just need to feed her and love her, and she will live," he continued, as if this was a matter of negotiation.

"Me and Dana even told her that we love her. And I made a wish with a flower."

"I don't know, Michael," I responded. "Sometimes these things happen. Sometimes newborn babies do not survive . . ." I trailed off, uncomfortable with the words that were struggling to come out of my mouth.

In that moment, I realized I felt helpless and afraid, so I was trying to rescue Michael and myself from the potential pain of losing the lamb. I also wanted to avoid the pain of seeing my beloved son's heart break from helplessness in the face of death.

I could see how my need to protect us led me to try to deny him the full experience when I told him, "This is how things are. Babies sometimes die."

In effect I was sending him the message that he should not feel afraid or helpless, because they are feelings of weakness, and that he should protect himself with reason. Part of me wanted him to avoid his feelings so his heart would not be broken.

But I was hit with the full awareness of the price of that protection! Did I want to disconnect him from his own humanity and vulnerability? To shut down his heart—where life itself resides—to protect him from pain?

No.

I did not want to protect him from his heartbreak. I wanted him to experience the aliveness, strength, and empowerment gained from being present with our hearts under all circumstances and from opening ourselves fully to any experience in the moment. How else can anyone truly live the life they were meant to live?

As I quickly became conscious of all this, I knew I wanted to change directions. I wanted to offer Michael the experience of being met where he was, of being understood and accepted for his feelings and needs in that moment.

How I long to offer this gift to my children on a regular basis!

And so I said to him, "Michael, my heart is touched deeply by how much you care about this little creature. I see how you want to protect her life. You are willing to do whatever is needed to save her, and I can imagine how helpless and distressed you feel when you neither have the certainty nor the power to decide what will be the end results of your efforts."

Michael's tears confirmed my understanding. He hugged me and cried quietly. I felt relieved and grateful for making this turn on time. I could support his efforts to connect with his feelings by offering my understanding of what it was like for him, instead of distracting him from his helplessness and fear, which would contribute to him adding a layer of protection to his heart. I remembered Marshall Rosenberg's words about learning to enjoy somebody else's pain. Finally, I got what he meant. It was the sweet pain of being with what was real, with being with What Is. For the first time ever, I enjoyed my son's tears.

As I sensed that Michael was feeling completely understood, I decided to offer him a piece of education.

"You know, Michael, I feel peaceful when I am doing everything that is within my power to show up for what matters to me, which in this case, is to care for life in all its forms and protect it as best I can. As far as I can tell, you are doing the same. We took the lamb into our house and offered her food, shelter, love, and care. I think this is all we can do. Whether she lives or not is not in our hands. And therefore, I'm letting go of being in charge of it.

"When I can let go of worrying whether my efforts will bring my desired results, I notice that I can focus my energy fully on responding to the situation with all the power I have to invite what I long for. Letting go of what I want to happen frees me to do whatever my heart is really moved to do in the situation, and therefore I have no regrets later on. Does this make any sense to you?"

"Yes, Aya, I'm doing everything I can. There is really nothing else to be done. And if she dies, I will bury her myself and I will look for the most beautiful stone to be put on top of her grave, so I will know where it is. Look at her, Aya. Isn't she beautiful?"

I nodded as we continued feeding the little lamb and petting her. She survived the night but died the next day.

Michael and Dan-Dan buried her in the backyard and placed a

wood sword that Dan-Dan made in preschool on top of it. It made a perfect cross.

On top of the sword Michael placed a pink crystal stone. I watched them from the porch as they leaned forward and silently sent the little lamb to her next journey with an open heart.

I stayed for a few more minutes, taking it all in, grateful for the rich connection, learning, and meaning we all took from the little lamb's short appearance in our lives.

—AYA CASPI, www.cnvc.org/aya-caspi

Empathy at Work

Creating a Culture of Compassion

One of my coaching clients, a computer engineer who consults on government projects, recently asked me about using empathy in her office.

"Why me?"

I hear this one a lot.

"Why should I have to do the extra work of empathizing with someone who's being unreasonable?" she asked.

"Do you want the quick answer? It's efficient," I said. "It's often the fastest way to get back on track when a collaboration has gone sideways, and someone's triggered."

She nodded and seemed satisfied. I knew she was ready to dig in.

Some workplaces have already created a culture that values compassion and connection. Thankfully, this is happening more and more as people realize the benefits of a compassionate workplace. Most professionals, however, need to understand how empathy is a useful and practical skill before they get on board. They need to understand all the ways it can improve their work and the bottom line.

I especially find that in stressed work cultures where people are constantly operating in crisis mode, it's hard for managers to understand why devoting time or money on cultivating soft skills in their teams would be useful. They might say, "Sure, in an ideal world we could spend resources on empathy, but it's not realistic for us right now." But that logic changes quickly when a forward-thinking manager recognizes empathy as an essential leadership skill that supports effectiveness and efficiency at work.

Empathy does many things, but at the core it lets people know they matter. When people have the sense that they matter—to coworkers, to clients, to superiors—it's easier for them to connect to their motivation. Work starts getting done more quickly and creatively. People begin looking forward to being at work.

It's easier for the workforce as a whole to embody the organization's mission when empathy is in the air.

In the following stories, you'll see examples of how people have used empathy skills in many ways and in different work cultures. You'll learn how executives, teachers, and committee chairs have used empathy to give others a voice. You'll also get a chance to see how leaders in powerful positions use empathy, both silently and out loud, as a point of leverage to support empowerment and encourage collaboration.

Practicing empathy isn't a panacea—it won't single-handedly shift an entire work culture. It will, however, create an opportunity to change key relationships in the office, which can then reverberate out. That's a good start.

*Empathy is a critical skill for
effective leadership for one, simple reason—trust.
If your employees don't trust you, you are not
a leader; you are just a manager. A key component
for building trust with others is empathy.*

—COLEEN KETTENHOFEN

New Employee Reviews

My first attempt to bring Nonviolent Communication into our workplace didn't go as well as I'd hoped. I wanted to introduce the concepts of consciousness, particularly needs awareness, but I hadn't found the right opportunity. I considered scheduling an introduction session for our team, but I worried people would roll their eyes at the term *nonviolent* and deflect, saying they're not violent people. I was also concerned that Nonviolent Communication, which had brought so much abundance and clarity in my life, might be received by my colleagues with resigned groans of compliance, defensiveness, or disinterest.

I remembered that employee reviews were coming up, so I thought I could use that as an opportunity to try something new with Nonviolent Communication. Our default review system was mostly useless, in my opinion, and I didn't have the impression that anyone liked it. I wondered if I could change our employee reviews to be more focused on needs.

After thinking it over, I landed on what seemed like a simple, yet perfect solution. I was so eager to test it out that I went to work the next day and tried my new approach on an employee, even though reviews weren't scheduled until the following week. This overzealousness could have been my first sign to slow down a bit.

I sat down with Mike and thanked him for being open to doing his review early. "We're going to try something a bit different this time," I said.

"It seems that way," Mike half-joked.

"You know, I've been wanting to bring Nonviolent Communication into the workplace, and I thought this might be a good opportunity."

I saw Mike stiffen at the word *nonviolent* as if it had triggered something. I thought, *I'm not off to a good start.* I realized he felt caught off guard because I'd requested this early review, and perhaps he was nervous because I'd introduced this new term without context. I felt like my perfect idea might be a terrible one.

"Sure," he replied.

"Hang in here with me," I said. "I've got a list with some universal human needs on it. I want you to scan this list and identify three needs that are being met right now for you at work and three that are not getting met. You got that?"

He paused. "Uhhhh . . . sure."

Mike scanned through the needs list with a pen in hand. He made check marks next to certain words and double check marks next to others. Meanwhile, I felt incredibly self-conscious and uncomfortable. It occurred to me that I hadn't thought through this idea at all. Perhaps offering an introductory session would have been a better plan. Ugh. I took a breath.

After a few minutes passed, he said, "You know, this is kind of difficult."

I regretted this whole endeavor, but I tried to muster some curiosity about where it could go.

"How so?" I asked.

"Well, I'm just not sure that it works this way. I'm not convinced that a need has either been met or not met. Sometimes things are organized to my liking, and other times they feel like a mess. That can happen in the same day, so I can't say my need for organization is either met or unmet. Also, organization isn't that important to me."

My throat was tight. "Right," I managed to say. Mike had a good point. I had lost sight of the point I was hoping to make.

"But," he continued, "I think there could be something interesting here. When I went through the needs list, I noticed a couple of big ones for me. I mean, a couple of these seem super important. I feel like I'd want you to know about them."

I relaxed a little and laughed to myself. Mike might understand this Nonviolent Communication thing better than I did.

"Tell me more," I said.

"Well, on a daily basis we have a bunch of different needs being met or unmet, and feedback about those needs could be useful in the moment. But in the long term, there might be a set of bigger needs that basically makes up who we are . . ." He trailed off, thinking. "Maybe it would help during an employee review if we could share our biggies with the team, so they could hear what needs are really important to us."

I stared blankly, thinking that my total blunder was turning into an unexpected learning opportunity.

"Like right now," he said.

"Go on." I was intrigued.

"Your needs for predictability and ease are probably not being met. But I'm not sure those are even important for you in the grand scheme of things. When I think about you, I see someone who is yearning to . . ." Mike looked at the needs list I had given him twenty minutes earlier. "Yearning to contribute and innovate."

Wow. I felt totally exposed, mushy, and vulnerable. But for the first time, I realized that Mike really got me on a deep level.

"Thanks, Mike. I feel really seen by you," I said, feeling stunned by how powerfully his words hit me.

"So maybe you could try this during the other reviews. Just ask people to share with you two or three needs that are super big for them in the workplace. They could look at the needs list and see what they respond to viscerally. See where it goes from there?"

I felt relieved and still somewhat foolish by how the meeting had unfolded. But I was also getting back on my feet, and I told him I thought his idea sounded excellent.

"This is kind of fun," Mike quipped. "I appreciate you 'hanging in there' with me on this. I think inclusion and trust are big for me, so thanks."

—JOSEPH MARTINEZ, www.nvcatwork.com

*Behind intimidating messages are merely people
appealing to us to meet their needs.*

—MARSHALL B. ROSENBERG, PhD

Doctors Under Pressure

Early one morning in an English hospital, I was setting up a communications course for young doctors. The slide projector wasn't functioning and four participants hadn't appeared yet. Two agitated doctors were not on my list but stood in front of me, convinced they had registered. Both had traveled from afar and were keen to join the course. I felt flustered. I dislike disappointing people who make an effort to attend. Moreover, I was late to start. I felt stressed.

I've led hospital trainings on dealing with conflict and complaints for ten years. I like supporting doctors who do crucial work under intense conditions. I also feel challenged by the context—time pressure, hospital hierarchy, and the harsh effects of health-service cuts. It's hard to convey the depth, subtlety, and potential of compassionate communication in one day. Doctors are used to condensed courses heavy on facts and directives, but a training course with space to reflect, feel, and intuit is novel.

My introduction was disrupted twice to welcome latecomers. After the half-hour no-show deadline, I invited the two hopeful doctors to join. Sweating, I tried to make up for lost time.

I usually start by empathizing with doctors who are required to attend these trainings by acknowledging the pressure to comply and the lack of choice. That day I covered it briefly.

I noticed the ratio of twelve women to four men in the room, with the men in a group at one side. After the first exercise, the doctor on the far end, Mark, began texting on his phone. Then Jackie's emergency beeper rang, which led to whispers and Jackie excusing herself. Doctors often have critically ill patients who they can't support while attending a training, which can be challenging for them and me.

Mark was sprawled low in his chair. He asked numerous questions as I outlined the needs-based communication model. I focused on responding carefully. Although my words were calm and clear, I felt flushed. My replies only helped in part. Mark voiced his opinions firmly.

"It's quicker and more efficient to just tell people what to do," he said. "Nicely, of course, saying please and thank you."

During a pause while they did a written exercise, I realized I had been answering the *content* of Mark's questions at face value, rather than drawing out the undercurrent that spurred his questions.

After a few exercises, Mark piped up, "This is like school. I already know how to communicate."

I tried to guess his perspective. "Is it hard to study something you've done all your life?"

He nodded, so I made other guesses. Did he want recognition for the people skills he already had? Perhaps he wanted to choose how to use his time? My empathy eased some tension, but I was still concerned his skepticism would be contagious, especially among the other men nearby. He and his friend Daniel muttered to each other the rest of the morning.

During the lunch break I hoped to catch Mark by himself, to help us connect and to dispel my brewing irritation. But I couldn't find him. During the afternoon session, Mark chatted off topic with two other doctors. I felt worried about him disrupting learning and spreading discontent. I felt like a swan, gliding on the surface but paddling frantically to stay on track. By now Mark was nearly horizontal.

Then he said loudly, "God, this is boring!"

Suddenly, I felt like laughing. I walked toward him and asked genuinely, "Are you fed up and frustrated?"

"Too right!" he replied.

"And wanting to feel more engaged, more alive?"

"Pretty much, yeah."

I continued to empathize by making similar guesses, and I began to feel more open and curious. I helped him take an interest in uncovering his boredom and discovering the values beneath it, especially autonomy and choice. He expressed anger about taking courses he had no time for, jumping through hoops to please management, the strain of shift work, and the unpredictability of poorly staffed wards.

As I relaxed, Mark revealed more. I abandoned my teaching timetable and became more present. He mentioned his pain over trying to heal a teenager who was unlikely to survive. He shared his fear of getting it wrong or causing harm. I empathized gently.

He also admitted he'd been poised to walk out. I suggested he was free to leave. As far as I was concerned, he had that choice. He shook his head, saying he was okay to stay for the last hour.

Mark grinned and glanced around the circle, saying, "I liked announcing I was bored. I couldn't say that to a consultant without dire consequences. Felt quite liberating!"

The other doctors seemed riveted as we connected. A few peers chimed in with their own struggles. The atmosphere had softened significantly. I wanted to end with a conflict resolution role-play, which involved me demonstrating first. I asked for a volunteer to play a patient's angry relative. Silence. No offers.

Finally, Mark sighed. "I might as well!"

Mark and I wore black hats to symbolize an angry, blaming mode. Mark's hot energy was palpable. Slightly daunted but enjoying myself, I took in his heat and his height, and I stepped into my reactive role. I removed my hat to represent a shift in me and reached across with a few empathy guesses, as Mark continued in the role of the raging relative. By understanding the fear, distress, and longing for respect in his role, the anger calmed. The demo ended to a ripple of applause.

In the closing circle, doctors shared their insights about the power of empathy and hidden human needs.

"The highlight was how unfazed you were under fire!" one doctor said.

Mark's friend Daniel said, "If you can handle Mark being so obstructive, these are great skills."

Another doctor said, "This stuff is pure gold."

I felt relieved, marveling at how the energy had shifted after I became more authentic and dropped my teaching agenda.

The last to leave was Mark, writing screeds on his feedback form. Then he crumpled the paper and threw it on the floor.

"I can't describe it all!" he exclaimed. "I'm still unsure about the model, but I'm glad I met you. I never knew boredom could be so interesting!"

On his way out, he smiled. "By the way, I don't think bossing people *is* the most effective way . . . Especially now that I see how much I mind about choice."

—VAJRASARA/ANNIE RANKIN, www.liveconnection.org.uk

Empathy before education.
Connection before correction.

—MARSHALL B. ROSENBERG, PhD

Misbehaving for the Substitute

The librarian of Lincoln Elementary School sent a note to Ms. Jackson, a third-grade teacher, who'd recently been out sick. She told her how noisy, rude, and disrespectful her class had been during their library visit with the substitute teacher.

When Ms. Jackson returned to school, she was curious to find out what had happened with her usually considerate students. I was there to help facilitate this discussion, using some of the tools from *The No-Fault Classroom* that we'd been introducing to the students.

Ms. Jackson had the students get their Feelings and Needs card decks from their cubbies. They hustled their way to the back of the room and grabbed their manila envelopes.

Ms. Jackson sat on a low chair, with her students arranged around her on the floor in a large circle. She read the librarian's note aloud.

"What does Ms. Ladd mean when she says you were noisy, rude, and disrespectful?" she asked. "What were you doing?"

The students, visibly concerned, blurted out their responses: *We talked a lot. Our voices were louder than they're supposed to be in the library. We didn't stop talking when the substitute teacher told*

107

us to. Some people drew on the bookshelves. We didn't put away our books, and somebody ripped up paper and left the pieces on the floor.

"Okay," Ms. Jackson continued, "think about what happened in the library. How do you feel about it now? Please go through your Feelings card decks and choose cards that describe the feelings that are coming up for you now."

Papers rustled purposefully, and students murmured quietly. They had sorted their feelings in this way many times during the year, and they were confidently selecting and placing cards on their mats.

Ms. Jackson went on when they looked ready. "So what needs did you have that were or were not met by what everyone did in the library? Please place your Needs cards on your mat." Their small hands deftly ruffled through the Needs card decks, stopping now and then to draw a card and place it on a mat.

"Who would like to share feelings and needs about what happened in the library?" she asked.

Molly looked at the cards in front of her and said she felt sad and embarrassed. Respect and cooperation were important to her, but she realized she hadn't been respectful or cooperative with the substitute teacher or Ms. Ladd. Juan agreed and said he was shocked the class had acted the way it did. Olivia jumped up to say she felt angry because she wanted to be heard and that she had tried to get people to stop, but no one would listen to her. Kim wasn't sure she wanted to say anything but then finally did.

"I want things to be fair," she said sadly. "We weren't fair to Ms. Ladd or the substitute."

The students had a lot to say, and this kind of sharing went on for several minutes. The talk was very general. No one was taking responsibility for what happened . . . or making accusations.

I leaned over to Ms. Jackson to make a suggestion. She turned back toward the students.

"When some kids were drawing on shelves, talking loudly, and dropping scraps of paper on the floor, what do you think their feelings and needs were?" she asked. "Can you think about what was going on for the people doing these things?"

The emotional floodgates suddenly opened. Before anyone had a chance to put cards on their mats, students began identifying themselves and excitedly sharing their feelings and needs. Jed said there were three classes in the library at once, and it was too hot and crowded for him. He said he was frustrated and upset that it was so uncomfortable, and that he would have to be there a long time. Heather admitted to ripping up a paper she had been given and throwing the pieces at the wastebasket. She saw that some pieces missed, but at the time she didn't care. She was impatient because she didn't know why the class was even in the library or what they were supposed to be doing. Aaron explained that he was doodling on the bookshelves because he felt discouraged and hopeless when he couldn't find the books he wanted, and there wasn't anyone to help him. It was in pencil and he meant to erase it, but he didn't have time.

After several more minutes of this kind of spontaneous, specific, heartfelt sharing, Ms. Jackson said, "I hear that some of you felt confused, uncomfortable, anxious, and frustrated. Is there more?"

"Shut down," shouted Chang. "There was no one to talk to about what was going on in me, so I just stopped listening."

"All right," Ms. Jackson replied. "So another feeling that came up is shut down. I'm hearing that these feelings came up because you wanted to be heard and to be clear about what to do, you had questions and needed help and support, you wanted understanding about what was going on in you, and you needed to be more comfortable in the library that was way too crowded and hot. Is there anything more?"

No one spoke.

"Now that you understand your feelings and needs, can you think of something you wish you had done instead of what you did?" Ms. Jackson asked.

Another wave of responses: *I wish I had picked up a book, sat in a corner, and read. I wish I had just worked on my homework. I wish I had asked if I could work in the hallway. I wish I had asked Jason to help me find the book I wanted. I wish I had drawn pictures on my own notebook paper instead of on the shelves. I wish I had walked over to the wastebasket and put the papers in.*

Ms. Jackson nodded and said, "Please, keep these ideas in mind next time you feel stressed and unable to tell anyone about your frustration. Now, with Ms. Ladd's note in mind, what shall we do next?"

Yet another floodgate opened, and everyone had something they wanted to do for Ms. Ladd: *Let's ask her what we can do to make it up to her. Let's write her a note. Let's make a pretty card to put it in. Let's have everyone sign it. Let's have her come to our room and someone can read the note to her here. Let's clean the bookshelves in the library. Let's have an appreciation party for her. Let's do all of those things! Let's write a note to the substitute teacher too.*

Excitement filled the air as students brainstormed about how to reconnect with both the librarian and the substitute teacher. Ms. Jackson divided them into groups to take on these tasks, and they spent much of the afternoon happily carrying out their plans.

—VICTORIA KINDLE HODSON, www.thenofaultzone.com

My . . . advice is to cultivate a sense of empathy—
to put yourself in other people's shoes—to see the
world from their eyes. Empathy is a quality of
character that can change the world.

—BARACK OBAMA

Difficult Personalities and Collaboration Breakdowns

My work with managers, executives, and business owners involves personal healing and what some call "inner game" work. Inevitably it extends to how people communicate at work—whether they can deliver honest and kind feedback, what said or unsaid things they hear when receiving feedback, and where limited collaboration skills hold them back. It's kind of like marriage counseling.

Jackson was a small business owner who partnered with a friend to launch a software start-up. The business plan revolved around a specific product, but Jackson's business partner, Doug, kept trying to pitch new ideas. This frustrated Jackson and prompted him to schedule a phone session with me, since I had been working with both of them individually, and occasionally as a pair.

"I've had to reign him in since before we opened our doors!" Jackson blurted just as soon as we said our hellos. "He's like a little kid, and I'm sick of it. We've got a plan. We just need to get in the black and stay focused for a few years. We can dream about expanding later. We're barely getting by right now."

I worried that the trust between Jackson and Doug was deteriorating. Jackson didn't want to cause waves, so he was nervous about verbalizing the tension he felt toward Doug about several small things. He kept telling himself to be nice, but his frustrations still leaked out.

Doug felt like Jackson was too black-and-white, too linear. Doug enjoyed the creativity of dreaming big and letting fresh ideas flow. He hoped Jackson would play along with these ideas. He didn't care so much about whether they followed up on certain ideas or tabled them for later. He just wanted to enjoy having an entrepreneurial spirit.

At the core of the conflict was that two business owners had different strengths to offer their organization. The challenge was that Jackson, the hard-working, linear thinker, did not value the creativity and the vibrancy his partner offered. And his partner was overlooking Jackson's gifts too.

Jackson had built up resentment around several issues, and he needed to vent. I asked him to talk freely while I listened. Once Jackson felt like I understood his point of view, his defensiveness softened, and we began prepping him to start a productive conversation with Doug. The goal was twofold. First, he wanted to speak his mind effectively, both frankly and compassionately. Second, he wanted to come out of the conversation feeling more connected to Doug, even if just a little.

I was there to support the conversation between the two business owners.

Jackson began by saying he wanted to touch base about some of their differences that affected the collaboration. He spoke carefully and clearly as he named his intentions.

"I think we both care a lot about this business. I know you're in it as much as me. I just want to talk a bit, so we can use our strengths better. Sometimes it seems like we work at cross-purposes unnecessarily."

"This is about that project suggestion I made the other day, isn't it?" asserted Doug, speaking much more quickly than Jackson had.

"Uh, no. Not just that. This is a bigger-picture issue. I just wanted to name a few things," replied Jackson, sounding flustered.

"Well, you never like my ideas. You brought me into this because of my background in sales, but you never want to hear my opinions about things!"

"This isn't about that . . . ," began Jackson, his volume increasing.

I spoke up and suggested we pause for a moment. Luckily, we had prepared for this. With a little help, Jackson switched gears into listening mode, which I think saved the conversation.

"Listen," I said, "it sounds like there are several things going on for both of you, so I'm really glad we're here to talk. Now, Jackson, I know you have certain things you wanted to say. But Doug may not have the space to hear them right now."

I stopped, smiling as I saw them each take a deep breath, which we had talked about before in our work.

Looking at Jackson, I asked, "Are you up for listening a bit? To see what's on Doug's mind?"

"Yeah," replied Jackson. "Sorry, Doug. Keep going."

"I'm getting fed up. I came into this as an equal, and now you just want to take over all the time. I never get any say. You just keep announcing what you want to do!" exclaimed Doug.

"Okay, so it's about being part of decisions?" asked Jackson, continuing to breathe deeply.

"Yes, that'd be nice!"

"It sounds like you want to have more say, like more input or collaboration?"

"Yes, I want more input. Of course! I want to be taken seriously!" Doug said, rolling his eyes.

Something snapped for Jackson and he snickered. "If you want to be taken seriously, maybe you need to make sure you come to all the meetings!"

Uh-oh. I clenched my teeth and waited to see if they could work it out.

"You know why I didn't come to that meeting! And I only missed one other, or maybe two. Man, it really pisses me off that you're bringing that up again."

"All right, I get it," Jackson said. "Listen, I'm upset, but I'm doing my best here. Sorry. I hear how annoying it is for you that I said that." He sighed and looked up.

Doug sighed in return. "Damn right. I can't believe you haven't let that go already. I've explained it so many times."

"So you're irritated and a little surprised to hear that come back up." Jackson was working hard. He rephrased it as a question. "Are you irritated I brought that back up?"

"Yes! But more than that, I'm not sure this is working out. You want me to be just like you, work your hours, and do things your way. I don't want to be judged by you all the time!"

Ah. Doug was essentially bringing up the topic that Jackson had wanted to dive into in the first place. We were circling around this core issue in their partnership. I was hoping not to get derailed by the smaller issues, which I thought were symptoms of a bigger problem.

"I get that," Jackson said. "I think I do, anyway. I'm hearing that you don't want to feel judged. That you want to know I appreciate your way of doing things. That I appreciate you."

"Yes!" replied Doug. "I took a bigger risk to do this with you. Well, in some ways bigger, in some ways smaller. But I don't want to stay in it if you don't listen to me."

"So . . . it's about me understanding what you contribute and wanting your contributions."

"Right." Doug's body posture softened noticeably.

"Well, I just want to say I do! I do appreciate you!" Jackson said. "I know I don't always handle it well when small things annoy me. And I admit I haven't been great about talking through every decision. But I want you to stay in it."

Doug nodded.

As if to fill the space, Jackson repeated, "I really do."

The conversation continued as the two spontaneously named various strengths they saw in the other. As a reality check, I weaved in some of things I'd learned during the individual work I'd done with them previously, briefly touching on personality-related challenges they were likely to continue having. We set up a schedule for more conversations in a way that felt collaborative. For example, "Let's see what we can do to figure this out." Rather than "How can I tell you everything that's wrong with you?"

I was happy and grateful that Jackson, in a pivotal moment, had listened when he really wanted to speak. The energy between them was more connected. I considered it a success.

—MARY GOYER, www.consciouscommunication.co

*We think we listen, but very rarely do we listen
with real understanding, true empathy.
Yet listening, of this very special kind,
is one of the most potent forces
for change that I know.*

—CARL ROGERS

Man-to-Man Empathy

In my work as a healthy lifestyle counselor at a large medical clinic, people often come to me for help managing their weight. One day, a well-dressed African American man in his fifties walked into my office.

As we discussed his weight-loss goals, I wondered what else in his life might affect the process of losing weight, so I asked him about stress. I learned that he had been through a harrowing experience just three weeks earlier. In a soft, calm voice, he described how his vehicle had been stopped by several police cars while on his way to an early morning shift. The police officers pulled him from his seat and held him facedown on the ground at gunpoint. He was released after some time, and in a blur, it was over. Since that incident, he had trouble sleeping and was feeling tense and upset. He hadn't told anyone because he worried his coworkers would tease him and he wanted to be strong for his family. He had seen a therapist twice, but it didn't seem to be helping.

I knew his story was important, so I sat, quietly at first, to respect his experience, and to honor that it was still affecting him deeply. Gently, I began to make guesses about how he might be feeling.

"EMPATHY NOTS"
Example

ADVICE

"Why don't you talk to her?"
"You might try . . ."

I said something like, "This was really shocking for you and maybe it's still got you shaken up a bit. Because, as a human being, you need safety—just basic safety. The shock of having guns pointed at you can stay with you for a while."

He nodded and tentatively agreed to that. "That's true. That makes sense."

Next, I asked about respect, wondering whether the treatment he experienced offended his sense of respect. He shrugged. I didn't see a shift in him, which often happens when an empathy guess really resonates.

I did, however, begin to feel something in my own body. I felt anger, maybe indignation. I imagined that if I had experienced the same thing, I would have trouble sleeping because I'd be mad. But he didn't express any anger at all. Not one iota. As a white male, that struck me, because I know that African American men experience a lot of disrespect and racism in our society. My guess wasn't on target, though, so I circled back around to ask about safety again.

"Well," he said, "what really bothered me was not so much about safety. I didn't think they would actually hurt me . . ."

My question prompted him to mention a new detail, though. When the shotgun was pointed at his head as he was lying on the ground, the policeman had cocked it. In a moment of insight, my client said he believed it was this memory that had kept him awake, tense and preoccupied.

I let this insight sink in and then something flashed in me, something strong. I felt an electric heat run through me, a deep and powerful physical sensation that filled me like fire; it almost made my hair stand up on end.

Suddenly, as this sensation surged through me, I felt sure I knew what the missing piece was. A word came to me, and I had to take a deep breath because tears were flowing. I said something like, "My brother, man to man, was this about dignity?"

He looked at me and tears filled his eyes. It was very uncomfortable and intense, but my guess was right. We sat suspended in that electric moment for several seconds. He nodded, and I felt a wave of power and honor and recognition and togetherness. We were together in the same understanding of what dignity really was.

We sat just like that. I remember shaking my head, holding my hands open, and saying, "Yes, yes." I felt three things wash over us—recognition, acknowledgment, and honoring of dignity.

As we let things settle, he seemed to shift. I followed his lead, accompanying him as he thought about what he could do.

I reflected this shift back to him. "Now that we know what this is about—dignity—you probably want to do something. Because everyone needs dignity. It's essential."

He agreed, straightening up in his chair. So we explored, gently, ways he might restore that dignity. One possibility was to open up to his wife and receive her care and understanding. Another idea was to write a letter to the police department to describe his experience, and maybe request some form of an apology. He imagined that some recognition would be helpful for his dignity. We talked about how the very act of writing a letter and honoring his own voice could restore a sense of power and agency. We had identified several possible action steps by the time we wrapped up our conversation.

He came back a week or two later like a different man. He talked about how happy he was about upcoming summer barbecues and family gatherings. He was more open and playful, though still soft-spoken and composed. He had talked to his wife and together they wrote a letter to the police department. They had not sent it, but writing it was enough. He thanked me for helping him. My attempt to be with him and show empathy had truly made a difference. Seeing the change in him was beautiful. I was inspired—it seemed like we both were.

—TIMOTHY REGAN, www.rememberingconnection.com

Most people do not listen with the intent to understand; they listen with the intent to reply.

—STEPHEN COVEY

Autonomy and Safety for Five-Year-Olds

I was in the middle of teaching an intricate music presentation at a Montessori preschool when I felt a little hand on my shoulder. Esetu, a five-year-old, wanted to know if she could use the kettle and microwave to prepare her lunch of noodle soup. I requested that she wait a few minutes so I could supervise her. I explained that I was concerned about her safety and would call her as soon as I was available.

When I got up a few minutes later to look for Esetu, I found that she had already used the kettle and her noodles were in the microwave. I quickly reached a level of blinding anger. *She didn't do what I asked. She doesn't care about what I say. She's irresponsible. I can't trust her.* I raged silently for a bit, and tried to get in touch with what was underneath my anger. Once I felt more relaxed, I was ready to talk.

I approached Esetu and asked if she would be willing to let me discuss something with her. She nodded. I knew if she wasn't willing, I'd be wasting my time.

"Esetu, I asked you to wait for me to supervise you before using the kitchen equipment, and then I walked in and saw that you had already used the equipment. This made me feel really scared because I care about you being safe from things like electrical shocks and burns. Can you tell me what you hear?"

Esetu responded by saying, "You think I'll hurt myself, but I KNOW how to do it! You showed me last time, remember?"

I replied, "Are you frustrated, or maybe hurt, because you'd like me to understand and appreciate that you can do it yourself?"

Esetu showed me a handful of fingers and said defensively, "I'm five! And I can do it!" She looked down at her feet.

I asked, "Would you like to be seen for what you can do?"

No response, so I tried again.

"So you're saying you can do this, but I won't let you? I guess that would be kind of confusing and annoying. You want to know if I understand and trust what you really can do?"

Esetu looked up with tears in her eyes and nodded yes.

"It really hurts when you think I don't trust you?" I continued. "Because trust is really important to you?"

Esetu climbed on my knee. Her body relaxed visibly, and she looked up at me.

"Would it be okay if I tell you what's going on for me?" I asked.

"Uh-huh," she said, still relaxed.

"I would like you to be supervised in the kitchen, not because I don't trust that you can do it, but because I need you to be safe," I said, making eye contact. "Could you tell me what you just heard me say?"

Esetu smiled and said, "You want me to be safe?"

The dialogue continued for a bit as we talked about sadness and how trust was important for both of us, even though we were going about it in different ways.

After we talked, Esetu had no further objections. She said she was willing to seek supervision before using the kettle, stove, or microwave.

—MATTHEW RICH

*The honesty that undergirds wisdom,
comes not from books or beliefs, dogmas
or doctrines, but from people.*

—ERNEST KURTZ AND KATHERINE KETCHAM

Discovering the Shared Experience of Home

As a professor, I supported a team of interaction design graduate students who were assigned the task of developing an app, product, or process to solve some kind of challenge in a local community organization. I listened while the students described their frustrating experiences of "hitting a wall" with their design project. They'd just returned from presenting research findings to the staff members of their partner organization, and the response had been lukewarm. Their slumped shoulders and glum faces spoke of disappointment and defeat.

The partner organization was a community resource center supporting the Bay Area's homeless population. They provided laundry and shower facilities, support services, meeting rooms, and a safe space to socialize and rest. The organization had encountered some communication struggles with their clients and were hoping for a "quick fix" to solve this dilemma, but the students didn't have a proposal yet.

"We've done our research and spent hours synthesizing our results, but we haven't had that a-ha moment to give us the direction we need," observed Jin.

"We can't seem to satisfy the folks at the center. They want us to improve their communication, but we're not sure what that looks like," added Dev.

"Who are we designing for?" Jeff asked. "The center's staff? The homeless clients? I'm not sure where to focus."

This team had initially been excited to work with people whose needs could be met with design solutions. In their Interaction Design Foundations course, they had learned that "empathy is the heart of the design process," and this was their first opportunity to exercise empathy in an applied setting.

I invited the students to share their experience and listened carefully as they described their research process and findings. The students recounted the hours they had invested in interviewing staff members, observing, attending staff meetings and events, and facilitating a workshop where they gained insights about the positive core of the organization.

They learned that staff members focused on making everyone feel welcome but felt overwhelmed by the large number of homeless clients they served. Staff members needed to get information to a growing number of clients, and they were frustrated that clients didn't read the fliers on the walls about the resource center's policies, case manager meetings, and other important events. Clients weren't showing up for scheduled events or making use of support services.

The students also showed me information they'd collected about the alarming number of homeless people living on the streets of San Francisco, and how stretched the homeless shelters were in trying to serve them.

When they were done reporting what they had learned, I said, "I hear that you've worked very hard on the design research. Now you're feeling confused about what you can offer the center's staff members to help them reach their clients in these demanding conditions. Is that right?"

"Yes!"

"We are so invested in this project. We want our design to work for everyone, but we really need to get on the same page," added Ryan.

"It sounds like your understanding is that the center's staff members want improved communication with their clients, and they'd like clients to read the important information posted on the walls. Do I understand that correctly?" I asked.

There were nods all around.

"I'm curious to hear more about how you've connected with the center's homeless clients. What have you learned about their needs?"

The students shared their discoveries about the center's clients. From one-on-one interviews, they'd learned that clients valued the center's services a great deal. Clients appreciated the opportunity to relax and connect with one another in the community room, and the women particularly liked the Thursday Ladies' Night gatherings. Clients emphasized the importance of having individual lockers, spaces they could call their own. One student noted that lockers were the only safe places where clients could store their personal belongings.

When asked about communications from the center, several clients said they never read the fliers covering the walls because they were chaotic and confusing. One client described the communications as "a tidal wave of overwhelming papers."

Estella turned to me and said quietly, "This project means so much to me. I spent three days at the center sitting with clients, asking about their experiences, and just listening. I used all the active listening skills we've practiced in class. I really connected with one of the clients, Anita. I was surprised that she wasn't much older than me. She said the center was the closest thing she had to a home, and her locker was the one space she could call her own. As I listened, I looked around the center and saw it in a different way. For the clients, it was home. I remembered what it was like when I first came to San Francisco and couldn't find a place to live. I moved from couch to couch in friends' apartments. I didn't have an address or a place to store my stuff. The only way people could find me was through my cell phone. It was a scary time. I realized that Anita and I shared a need for a safe place that we could call home. I want our design project to help clients feel at home in the center."

Everyone was silent. I said, "It sounds like you were deeply touched by your time with Anita. I hear that you really want to support her with your work at the center."

"Yes, oh yes!" Estella exclaimed, leaning forward with excitement. Then she stopped. "But I thought our project was to design a communication system for the center, not the clients."

I looked around the table, and the students looked back at me expectantly.

"What I'm hearing is that you've been hard at work researching the staff members' needs because you understood that was the assignment. In the process, you've also come to understand and care about the clients, and you want to support them as well. Is it possible to design a communication solution that meets both of their needs?"

There was an almost audible click. Several students started talking at once, describing their interactions with clients during the previous weeks. We learned that clients really appreciated that center staff members knew them by name, and that clients had special locations where they could leave each other notes. Jin showed us a photo of the inside of a client's locker with photos of his family and dog. Students shared their surprise in learning that almost all of the clients had cell phones and relied on them for communication—just like the students did.

Once they shifted toward sharing the experience of being at home with the center's clients, the students' minds and hearts opened and they began brainstorming best practices for communicating at home. They were able to use empathy to find solutions for meeting multiple needs. During the next several hours, the students put themselves in the clients' position and sensed that they wouldn't want papers covering their living room walls. They put themselves in the staff members' position and felt the urgency of getting an important message to a roommate they cared about. The students remembered communication methods they'd worked out in shared housing situations, and they began sketching a phone app that staff members could use to get personalized communication to their clients.

The students prototyped several communication designs and presented them to the center's staff members and clients, who enthusiastically engaged in making modifications and adding new elements to the designs. The team collaborated with the center to organize and significantly reduce posted fliers. They co-created locker mailboxes and an electronic system to personalize printed communications for delivery to locker mailboxes. They developed a customized phone app that solved many of the center's communication challenges. It enabled staff to send important news to clients, enabled clients to send messages to staff and sign up for events, and provided a venue for clients to send messages to each other.

The students became dedicated members of the center's community and spent hours with clients to help personalize the interiors of their lockers. In the end, everyone felt more at home.

—SHARON GREEN, www.wisedesigncolab.com

It's harder to empathize with those who appear to possess more power, status, or resources.

—MARSHALL B. ROSENBERG, PhD

Executive Bully

I was in a meeting with Patty, a manager from a different department than mine. I didn't know her well, but she seemed dynamic and innovative. I began to explain some project limitations I was worried about. As I shared my perspective from a technical point of view, Patty's responses became louder and more pointed. She seemed adamant and angry, as if my sharing of information came across as insubordination. I tried to express my intention to collaborate on a solution, but she kept stopping me mid-sentence, saying things like "You need to do this" or "No excuses" or "Just make it work." Finally, I simply said, "Yes," and left the office quickly.

I felt surprised and shaken, especially since what had triggered her seemed neutral to me. The story in my head about Patty started taking shape. She was irritable and erratic. I soon discovered I wasn't the only one who felt this way. Many people who worked closely with Patty felt similarly. She had a reputation for being a bully and for embodying all the qualities you *don't* want in a manager.

After that meeting, I walked on eggshells around Patty. I tried to dismiss and condemn her, but that didn't make my internal state any better. So I actively tried to explore my own vulnerability related to her. This was hard because my self-judgments were that I was weak and oversensitive. I decided to be honest with myself, realizing that I felt pain because I cared.

I could also see that I deeply wanted peace with her (as I do with all people). I knew a peaceful relationship might not be possible, but once I developed respect and compassion for the part of me that wanted a good relationship with her, I had more tolerance for the fact that it wasn't entirely within my control. After working on it for months, I got to the point where I felt at ease in Patty's presence. Meanwhile, colleagues complained about how difficult Patty was and how she was destroying the company. She was becoming "The Cause of All That Is Wrong" according to the office narrative. I thought the stories oversimplified the situation and left out other dynamics at play.

Shortly thereafter, I discovered that Patty had emailed her staff. "I've heard rumors that I'm difficult to work with. I've heard people say I've done things that were hard on them, but no one has ever confronted me about it. I can't address something that I don't know about."

I noticed a strong impulse to talk to her. It felt like a natural continuation of all the inner work I had done. This was an opportunity to heal the company I cared about. But I also I wondered if I was delusional. *Would it matter? Could I really make a difference?*

I spoke about it with a coworker, Sheila. After I mentioned what I was considering, she responded, "This is scary because you don't know what will happen. You might become her number one enemy. On the other hand, the reason we make progress in the world is because of people willing to do scary things out of faith and hope."

Sheila continued to paint the larger context of what it can take to change the world or our small piece of it. As she spoke, my focus shifted from feeling delusional about facilitating change in our organization to asking whether I had the courage to try.

The next day, a golden opportunity came. Patty approached me after a meeting and said, "I have a feeling that I've hurt you. If there is anything I've done, I'd love it if you could talk to me about it." It was a direct request. It felt sincere and vulnerable. I wanted to be savvy about the fact that I was about to give difficult feedback to someone higher up, so with the support of a neutral witness, we agreed to chat.

I began by saying, "I want to explain why I agreed to meet with you. I was touched by your desire to check in and hear me out." I paused and took a breath. "I want to acknowledge that this meeting is scary for me because you have more power in this organization that I do. But I sense your sincerity. If I can help you understand some aspect of this dynamic so that you can improve yourself or your relationships, that is very meaningful to me. I believe very firmly in the innate goodness of every human being and the possibility of change."

"This is very good to hear. Did I do something to offend you?" Patty asked.

With a deep breath, I said, "Every human being is a mixture of positive and negative qualities and sometimes we're not aware of the impact we can have on each other. A few months ago, during a meeting about a project, we had a conversation. This is what I remember of it . . ." I went on to tell her what I remembered her saying. I explained how her responses seemed to use a lot more force than what seemed necessary for the situation.

"I don't remember any of this at all," she replied. "I'm sorry I said something that hurt you."

I thought about a conversation I'd had with my therapist in which she'd told me it's common for bullies to be out of touch with the ways they affect people around them. In light of that, her response was understandable. I offered her some empathy.

"I imagine it's painful to hear that you had a negative impact," I guessed.

"I don't understand why other people have talked behind my back. Why didn't you approach me earlier?" asked Patty.

Rather than answer directly, I chose to guess at what was really behind the question. "Are you wishing you'd had a chance to address these situations instead of hearing them indirectly?"

"Yes!" she exclaimed.

"It sounds like you wish people were more considerate of your feelings?"

"Yes. This has been really hard on me," she said, taking a deep breath.

I continued my empathy guesses. "I appreciate you for listening and taking this in. It's not easy to hear difficult things about yourself."

"Yes, this is surprising but helpful," Patty replied.

Then I switched gears, saying, "This incident was really hard on me, and it took me a while to get over it. I didn't consider talking to you about it because your actions seemed so erratic and severe. I didn't trust your ability to be caring. I'm not telling you this to make you feel bad, but to help you understand it had an effect. I avoided you, and it took a lot of work on myself to get to the point where I felt okay in your presence."

"Wow, a lot of work on yourself? I'm so sorry." The sadness and surprise on Patty's face was evident.

"Yes. I can see that you're really sad about what I experienced with you. It helps me feel better," I said.

"I'm glad." She seemed touched.

"And I also take responsibility for the fact that no one can ever know for sure what someone's intention is . . ."

"Yeah," she agreed. "Sometimes people are too sensitive."

"Yes, some people would have taken it better than I did and some would have taken it worse. But listen, your actions during our meeting were egregious. I understand that you don't remember this particular incident between us, but there are others who have found communicating with you difficult."

This was a tender and delicate line. I didn't want her to beat herself up, but I wanted her to face up to the effect she had on me and others in the organization who didn't have the courage to speak.

She seemed to be taking it in.

I went on: "I completely agree there's an element of personal responsibility in any dynamic, but it's also true we affect each other. I imagine there are some people in your life who have influenced you in a positive way, maybe even inspired you. True?" I asked.

She nodded.

"And some people have negatively influenced you. How we interact with people encourages them to bring out their best or their worst. Am I making sense?"

"Yes," she replied.

"I want you to shine at your job. I can see that you want good relationships with the people you work with. I hope if you understand my experience, it will help you calibrate how you act and be more successful."

"I can tell that you care, and I appreciate this," she said.

At the end of our conversation, Patty let me know how much she valued my frankness. I realized later that the courage to speak with her grew out of the same vulnerability that I had held so many self-judgments about. The part of myself that Patty hurt was also the part that cared. The part that cared enabled me to open up to her and see her good qualities, despite her challenging behavior. I could say difficult things with love and respect.

In the months that followed, I heard through the rumor mill that Patty reigned in her temper considerably. I was sad, however, that she seemed muted compared to her old self. I hope in time, she learned how to speak kindly and respectfully while preserving her authenticity and passion. I regret that I didn't offer more empathy and support, but I also appreciated how I showed up, considering all I was juggling at the time: my aspirations and tenderness, the scope of my communication skills, her discomfort, and my career.

All in all, I'm pleased with the progress we made that day, and all the work that went into it.

—PHOENIX SOLEIL, www.phoenixsoleil.org

Empathy lies in our ability to be present.

—MARSHALL B. ROSENBERG, PhD

Skeptical Hospital Administrator

A hospital hired my partner and me to help them with some staffing problems. The emergency room was a mess at the hospital. They estimated losing more than $350,000 in turnover costs because the nurses and doctors weren't getting along. They reported daily drama in this work culture, and a lot of employees had quit over the course of time.

The hiring and training budgets were high, so the hospital executives wanted to find solutions to the staffing problems. We gave about six hours of training to the emergency room staff, with some basic tools for connection and cooperation. In the eight months following the introductory training, the hospital's turnover costs plummeted to almost zero. So they hired us to come back and teach other classes.

One class in particular was set up for the entire leadership team, including the board of directors, all senior managers, and every executive in the hospital. Attendance was mandatory, which wasn't ideal given the role that choice plays in what we teach.

As we arrived, I noticed a woman in the front row who didn't look happy about being there. Although she sat up front, which is often a good sign that there's curiosity and interest in the class, everything else about her body language said *no, no, no*. She held her arms crossed, her legs crossed, and sat with her body twisted away from us. For the first part of the day, she didn't even look at us once.

I guessed that her behavior was emblematic of the hospital culture, but rather than try to connect with her directly about not wanting to be there, we empathized—out loud—about what it's like to be in a situation where you're telling yourself you have to do something or get punished. This became part of our training and weaved in well with our content on collaborating. We wanted folks to understand that whenever any of us have the idea that we *have to* do something, we're living in what we call "jackal" consciousness, a space of life-alienating communication, and it's as if we're under the spell of threat.

My partner and I spoke about these ideas in general and began to move through the deceptively simple process we teach around self-empathy, in which people get the opportunity to transform "obligation" energy and begin connecting to their own needs.

As we proceeded through the exercises, we noticed the woman in the front row beginning to shift toward her own needs. She appeared to be following our suggestions about giving herself empathy, and as she self-empathized, it seemed like she became more connected to her motivations. Everything about her body language relaxed. As the day wore on, not only did she shift her body language, she engaged us with questions and challenges about our training content. It was great to see how dynamic the discussion became.

It was tempting at times to move into education-mode, to correct some of the ideas she might have misunderstood. Instead, we continued showing empathy by acknowledging her experience and connecting with her by saying things like "So for you, it's a real concern that these communication tools will make things inefficient. Yeah. Got it."

We were happy to answer questions she had, but we never tried to convince her of anything. We simply stayed with what was important to her when she brought up a concern, then went back into the material for the group.

At the end of the day, I was surprised by her warm and heartfelt hug. What a transformation! We'd made a true connection—and we had the sense that we'd offered her at least a few ideas that she would make tangible use of!

—JIM MANSKE, www.radicalcompassion.com

*Intellectual understanding of a problem blocks
the kind of presence that empathy requires.*

—MARSHALL B. ROSENBERG, PhD

Earning His Certificate

At the end of our last Nonviolent Communication class, a man incarcerated in San Quentin State Prison asked me why he did not receive a certificate. I reminded him that our class agreement included several homework and attendance agreements, which he had not kept. He objected at first, saying that I had not been clear about the expectations. Then he argued that he had done the work, which my records showed no indication of. He spoke more quickly and raised his voice louder and louder as we talked.

At some point, I realized my own voice was getting louder and faster as I answered him. This has become a signal to me that I have entered a "who's right" argument, which never goes anywhere useful, and that I've left behind the things underlying the argument that each person cares about.

I remembered that when people raise their voices and speak faster, it often indicates a growing urgency to be heard. So I stopped and said, "I notice that my voice is getting faster and louder, and it sounds like yours is too. Let me pause for a minute and see if I can understand what is important to you about what you're saying. Can you tell me why this certificate is important to you?"

Immediately, he calmed down a little and told me, "Look, I don't care if there is a certificate in my file for the judge or for the parole board. That doesn't matter to me. But I have never gotten a certificate for anything in my life. I want to be able to put it up on the wall to look at, knowing that I did something and that someone saw me do it."

Hearing his longing moved me. "So it sounds like what matters to you here is acknowledgment, accomplishment, and maybe even knowing you matter?" I paused a moment while he took this in. "And perhaps you even want self-respect when you look at a certificate? I'm really touched as I connect to what you said."

He seemed almost relieved to hear I was getting it. "Yeah, exactly."

"Totally. I got it. I also want to align with my value of integrity," I said. "I want to know that when I give someone a certificate of completion, it means something I can stand behind in terms of growth, self-responsibility, and partnership in learning. I want to see if we can find a way to meet your needs and mine too," I said. I paused to see if he seemed ready for me to shift gears.

"What about this as an idea?" I asked. "I will put a note in your prison file saying you are *not* receiving a certificate of completion, but I will make you a certificate of participation. What do you think?"

"Yeah!" he said. "That sounds really good!" He was completely happy with this plan. We left with mutual positive regard and respect.

If this scenario had gone a different way, he may have left feeling bitter and resentful, possibly bad-mouthing the Nonviolent Communication class to other inmates. I might have left with a sense of how uncooperative and belligerent he was. Instead, I walked away that day feeling tenderness around our shared humanity.

—MEGANWIND EOYANG, www.baynvc.org

Judgments, criticisms, diagnoses,
and interpretations of others are all alienated
expressions of our own needs and values.
When others hear criticism, they tend to invest
their energy in self-defense or counterattack.
The more directly we can connect our feelings
to our needs, the easier it is for others
to respond compassionately.

—MARSHALL B. ROSENBERG, PhD

The "Difficult" Client

I was working with a dream team on web marketing for a major high-tech company in Silicon Valley. We loved what we did, and we were good at it, if the Webby Awards on the shelf counted as evidence. In my role as project manager, I had lots of responsibility but little authority. I didn't mind, because I loved to collaborate . . . well, usually.

Our client, Sean, was working on a new venture that he insisted was "the next big thing." With great excitement, he proclaimed, "We need a new web presence—something splashy, with a big 'wow' factor. When can you have it done?"

He seemed quite naive about how it all worked. His enthusiasm was endearing but a bit overwhelming. He reminded me of a three-hundred-pound puppy.

"Well, first here's what we need from you," I said, mentioning a few items that would affect our timeline. "Once you've pulled together your documentation, let's schedule a team meeting to kick things off."

A few days later, he said he was ready. We gathered as a team, but Sean showed up empty-handed. We reviewed again what we needed from him.

"If you need outside help pulling it together, let us know. We have people we can recommend," I offered. He seemed perplexed.

Sean continued to call, badger, and plead for project information without offering any of the documents that we needed. He was tenacious, which I had appreciated up to a point.

He resorted to threats. He said he was would escalate things and "out" our whole department—highlighting me as the roadblock. His attacks on me felt personal. *Is this what bullying feels like?* I wondered.

My resistance grew, and I lost my appetite to work with him.

Then Sean emailed me to say he had publicly announced the date when the "next big thing" would be available. I was blindsided. Our backs were against the wall. Not having a website up was not an option, so there was no turning back. Sean had committed our team to a launch date without even consulting us.

I was furious. "What was he thinking?" I screamed under my breath.

Time to slow down and take a deep breath. I recalled that if I could find some thread of connection with him, even just within myself, I'd feel better. But I struggled to connect with him because so many things about him rubbed me the wrong way—his pushiness, his demanding style, his incompetence.

These were all great clues about what was important to me.

I placed my hand on my heart and let myself really feel the frustration and disappointment, the yearning for consideration, and the desire for respect for our team's expertise.

From this more self-connected place, I felt a twinge of curiosity. *What might be going on for him?* I understood that this project was really important to him. I guessed he really wanted to do well, in ways that mattered to him. I could relate to that.

Still, I struggled. I didn't trust that he'd act in good faith. He'd been aggressive, unreliable, and unpredictable. I couldn't imagine us sitting down to talk about how to work better together. I recognized my narrow-mindedness and I just didn't like him.

Through my distress, I saw how much I longed for care, consideration, reliability, predictability, and clear communication. I wanted these for him and for me.

I saw this disagreement as a chance to deepen self-connection, to reaffirm my own values around work, and to act with integrity about what was meaningful for me. I focused on how to move this project forward despite the inherent challenges. I felt more creative and resolute. I noticed that I suddenly wasn't taking him so personally.

Later that week, my team and I met with Sean. Seven of us squeezed into a small office. The room was tight, the air thick with anticipation.

I began, "Sean, I know we've had challenges. I get that the stakes are high for you, and you've got a lot riding on it. I know you were hoping for something splashy for your launch."

He nodded in agreement.

From a place of clarity and calm, I shared the constraints we were up against. It really wasn't personal.

Sean was quiet. For the first time, he seemed pensive and understanding.

Unexpectedly, he brightened and said, "I can tell you've put a lot of thought into this. I know I haven't been easy to work with. How do we move forward from here?"

Finally, we were on track.

—ANN OSBORNE

Instead of offering empathy, we often have a strong urge to give advice or reassurance and to explain our own position or feeling. Empathy, however, calls upon us to empty our mind and listen to others with our whole being.

—MARSHALL B. ROSENBERG, PhD

One Versus the Committee

I was asked to sit on a hiring panel for our special education department. We were looking for candidates for several new positions, including an instructional assistant who would work in a specific classroom all day alongside the main teacher.

After we interviewed three candidates for the instructional assistant position, we had an opportunity to discuss our impressions with another panelist, Roy. He was the main teacher who would work alongside the assistant.

I was surprised to learn that Roy was leaning toward the third applicant who had not stood out to me at all. In fact, she'd performed so poorly during the interview, one panelist thought she'd deliberately sabotaged it. Her answers to the interview questions were short and vague; they didn't inspire much confidence.

Every person on the panel, other than Roy, took turns sharing reasons why they felt the third applicant was not qualified to work with special education students. But as we continued to talk about the other two applicants, and the qualities they displayed during their interviews, he kept going back to how strongly he felt about hiring the third applicant.

Now, we were all aware he had a higher stake in the decision because the new person would work directly with him all day. I also knew he had a good impression of this applicant because he'd worked with her before and he knew the stronger qualities that she had exhibited as a substitute instructional assistant in his room. We all understood that, but following his reasoning was difficult because we were required to make hiring decisions based on the evaluation tools we had.

As we weighed the importance of organizational skills and interpersonal skills needed to work with students, he seemed to contradict himself. First, he said his top choice applicant could learn the skills, then later he said the skills couldn't be easily taught.

After several rounds of discussion going late into the afternoon, I sensed that Roy was defensive and angry. He was agitated by our clarifying questions as we tried to make sense of his opinions. At that point, I finally realized he was coming from a place of fear, based on what I knew about the history of his program.

"Are you nervous that you'll get someone worse than applicant three, who at least you already know?" I asked.

"Yes, exactly," Roy replied, throwing up his hands.

"Okay," I said. "So you're afraid that whoever gets hired might turn out to be as challenging as—or maybe even more difficult than—the people from last year?"

"Yes!" he exclaimed. "We cannot go back to where we were last year. We have to be better!"

Everyone at the table nodded and sat quietly for a moment. We knew the interviews were taking place months later than they should have, because of circumstances beyond anybody's control. What we hadn't discussed was how this might be contributing to the difficulty of finding good people for these positions.

"We get that. We totally agree," said one panelist, and then gently reiterated their concerns about applicant three. This time it seemed like Roy really heard them. I sensed that we were on the same page, but still frustrated because no one felt excited about any of the applicants.

After a minute of silence, someone suggested that we interview a fourth person who couldn't be there that day. Everyone agreed to that idea. We came up with a plan to meet the fourth applicant and then reconvene for more discussion.

By letting him know I truly cared about his program, I sensed that Roy felt like we got him, that we understood his concerns, and it had transformed the conversation.

The next morning, we returned, and he was ready to change his mind. We interviewed the fourth person later that day—and that person was dynamite! We were ALL sold! It felt good to see how it all played out. I was glad there was cohesion around the decision, and that no one on our panel had the experience of not being heard.

—KEVIN GOYER, www.consciouscommunication.co

People who are emotionally adept—who know and manage their feelings well, and who read and deal effectively with other people's feelings—are at an advantage in any domain in life, whether in romance and intimate relationships or picking up the unspoken rules that govern success in organizational politics.

—DANIEL GOLEMAN

Salary Negotiations and Women's Empowerment

Advocating for my salary has always been crucial to me throughout my career as I accepted roles in new organizations. For every job offer, I pushed for a higher salary, knowing that women make less than men (seventy-two cents for every dollar their male counterparts make), generally take care of our kids and our elderly, and live longer lives. Women's inequality, and our huge lack of resources throughout our lives, has always been a concern of mine—so salary negotiation is part of my activism.

When I first applied to a local nonprofit, the listed salary was low, unfeasibly low. On the other hand, I was excited about the position they offered, and I wondered if I could make the position work for me in terms of financial sustainability. They were open to having a conversation about the salary and, as we talked, we began

144

to reconceptualize the job to include higher-level responsibilities, which would increase the salary.

I could see the executive director was stretching to make the offer work for me financially. She was already going higher than the top of the original range—but it still wasn't enough. This was a huge pay cut compared with the positions I'd held for the previous fifteen years, low enough that it would be a challenge to support myself financially.

When they offered a new salary, I decided to be frank. "I can't accept the job for that amount. I'm sorry. I really need to make a higher salary and work fewer hours."

Mandy, the executive director, replied, "Well, we've already done what we can on our end. It's really the best we can offer for this role."

"You've already stretched in a number of ways," I acknowledged.

"Right," said Mandy. "We just don't have the budget for more."

"I'm guessing that as a nonprofit, you have more financial struggles than other organizations. And I recognize that, in the arts, pay is lower than in other kinds of nonprofits because arts are generally not supported in this country."

"Exactly," Mandy replied with a nod and a slightly softer voice. "We do our best, but it can be rough."

"Mmm-hmm. You do what you can do."

"Exactly," she repeated. "Actually, our original intention was to hire someone on the low, entry-level end of the range for this job. So we have already come up for you, in a few ways."

"Right, so you initially had a different plan in terms of your hiring strategy. I get that. It sounds like you've shifted a lot in response to me. Is that kind of what you're saying?"

"Thank you, yes," she affirmed.

I paused and then switched gears. "I really do get that. I also would like to share my values as a woman, if you don't mind, and how important it is that I advocate for myself as a woman. Do you mind if I say a thing or two about that?"

"Oh, of course!" exclaimed Mandy.

"Thank you. Because of the reality of pay disparities between women and men, I feel it's important to really stick with this conversation about compensation, both in terms of benefits and salary. It's one thing I can do about this larger social issue."

I finished my thought and, as I took in what looked like surprise on her part, I took a deep breath to calm my stomach.

"Sure," she sputtered. "That's fair. I mean, I want you to know we are a largely female-run organization here. We're family friendly. We go out of our way to give people time off to have babies and we make it easy for our staff to have their kids here. There's a changing room adjoining the bathroom, for example. There are a lot of things I've been trying to do to make it a family-friendly place."

As she continued speaking, she referenced some of the statistics about women's economic inequality that let me know she deeply understood my bigger point. That made me want to keep connecting.

"I'm really getting all the ways you try to support families and the women who work here. You named a number of things you're paying attention to, including the bigger picture about women and money," I reflected.

"Yeah! It's important!" she exclaimed.

"Agreed. Okay, well let's keep going, then."

"Right. Well, I'll review parts of the benefits package," Mandy continued. "We give two weeks of vacation. We have an excellent health care plan, which we cover completely. We have excellent dental and vision care. Those are fabulous. We give a free week of vacation during the holidays, which people love. . . ."

"One second," I interrupted. "I'd like to ask for three weeks of vacation. Is that on the table?"

She shook her head, saying, "Well, we do give that free week at Christmas . . . That's really it."

"So I'm hearing that a third week of vacation isn't viable, but that there is a third week built into this holiday time off. Is that right?" I asked.

"That's right."

I continued focusing on reflecting her words back to her, asking questions, naming key points important to me. I also named when I could see we were on the same page about some of our wishes. When we took a break from the conversation, I left without a sense of how it would all turn out, but I felt happy with the energy of collaboration I felt between us.

Mandy came back with an extra $5,000 more than the original offer, and she proposed a significantly shorter work week. That felt really good. I felt proud that I had pushed and negotiated, with what seemed like the right amount of pressure. I sensed they were really stretching, as was I. When I asked that we review it again in six months, I got a yes on that too.

So I accepted.

Mandy, my new executive director, took me aside later and said, "Gosh, I have *never* advocated for my salary when going for a new role. And, come to think of it, no woman I've interviewed has ever negotiated for a higher salary before you. I totally respect that you took a stand, and I see why, as a woman, it's so important."

Stunned, I tried to take her acknowledgment in, but it was hard for me to hear. It seemed sad to me.

My immediate boss, also in the room, echoed Mandy's experience. "Me neither. I've never negotiated in my life, or had another woman negotiate with me. I'm impressed that you did!"

I'm glad I said what I said in those initial meetings, and that my bosses were impressed. Being able to express my understanding of Mandy's concerns supported us in working together around some of my bold salary requests, and that served me well. However, I also think it's important to say that using empathy skills at work is not a panacea. Our organization continues to be underresourced, perhaps dysfunctional, and my relationship with my executive director is incredibly challenging despite my regular attempts to connect. Sometimes I wonder if I did the right thing by accepting the role.

Nonetheless, I hope more women will follow suit by stepping into their power, especially in these key conversations. Perhaps it's easier to do so knowing that power doesn't have to come at the expense of connection. Quite the opposite—connection and empowerment go hand in hand.

—DEANNA ZACHARY, www.nvcsantacruz.org

Contrary to what most people believe, trust is not some soft, illusive quality that you either have or you don't; rather, trust is a pragmatic, tangible, actionable asset that you can create.

—STEPHEN COVEY

Agile Team Trust and Emotional Safety

I coach teams to collaborate more effectively, inspired by the Manifesto for Agile Software Development, which is a set of methods and practices based on specific values.

The first shared value is to put individuals and interactions over processes and tools—to respect people, create emotional safety, honor the relationships, encourage face-to-face conversations, and give the teams autonomy to design solutions. We value collaboration as the most effective way to develop software.

As a facilitator, I start our daily planning meetings with a brief check-in period when each person shares something about their personal lives and I offer empathy, reflecting the heart of what I hear. This daily ritual helps to create trust and mutual respect within the team. Establishing this trust from the get-go is essential, so when a team needs help, they already trust me to represent them. I can step in and act quickly to support their product delivery goals, which they want to do well to please their customers.

A few weeks after starting on a multi-team project, I began hearing about a manager named Frank who was interrupting teams and acting like a bully. Using the Agile Manifesto methods and principles, we let teams focus on delivering what they agreed to do during a "sprint." In a sprint, teams receive the time, resources, and support of short coordination meetings to help them complete a tangible task. But Frank was scheduling long meetings in the middle of sprints to check on things, instead of waiting until the end. Even after I suggested stopping these mid-sprint meetings, I later learned they continued in secret.

One day, Manfred came to my office to tell me about a mid-sprint interruption that had occurred the previous night. He seemed horrified as he described Frank's behavior. Manfred shared how Frank had grilled each developer, asking them about the status of their tasks, and then he interrupted them repeatedly as they tried to answer his questions.

Frank had asked a developer, "What's the status of this task? Is it done or not?" As the developer began to explain, Frank interrupted saying, "I asked you a yes or no question." The developer tried to repeat his explanation, only to be cut off by Frank again.

Manfred mentioned other check-ins that went similarly. "Buddy, your information is not useful to me. I don't want to hear that. Is it done or not?"

Manfred was notably upset.

I didn't know how to proceed until Sally, a bright technical leader came to me, saying, "Frank is a bully!"

"Oh," I said. "Are you scared because you don't have the safety to speak?"

"Everyone is scared!" she replied. "No one is able to explain

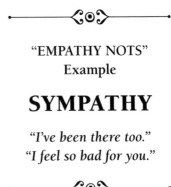

"EMPATHY NOTS"
Example

SYMPATHY

"I've been there too."
"I feel so bad for you."

themselves. He even makes us generate reports mid-sprint to show the status of our tasks. And then proceeds to tell us how to do our jobs."

I was shocked because agile software development is about both mutual respect and efficiency. Creating reports during a sprint is considered a total waste.

"Gosh, no respect and wasteful?" I asked.

"Yeah! Frank even said he had the right to fire us. It's so bad, our managers are even scared of him. No one is looking out for us. We really need your help!" she finished, with a big sigh.

I was dumbfounded. I had no experience dealing with a manager who openly threatened people.

In the end, my sense of justice and protection drove me to escalate the issue to the client's upper management team. Eventually, the human resources department got involved and Frank was reassigned to a different role.

The daily check-in period with my team where I practiced empathy was the catalyst for team trust and emotional safety, which contributed to program-wide respect and collaboration. This, along with other aspects of agile software development, led to efficiency in producing deliverables every two weeks—and happy customers.

—ANONYMOUS

If you want others to be happy, practice compassion.
If you want to be happy, practice compassion.

—DALAI LAMA

Master Teacher

I learned basic algebra in the eighth grade from a teacher who possessed finessed skill in working with teenagers. Everything ran well under his watch. As a kid, I took it for granted, of course. But I remember several occasions in which Mr. Beyta chose compassion in our classroom, by expertly redirecting misbehaviors without making a big deal about them.

He was a math guy, obviously—not a warm and fuzzy type— yet we all knew he cared. As I look back on a particular memory, I realize just how much empathy I received from Mr. Beyta one day, even though it took me years to recognize it.

I remember sitting in his class, gazing out the window one afternoon. It was after lunch, I was a little spacey, and I didn't realize I'd said, "Those clouds are massive," out loud until the whole room turned to look at me.

"Goyer," he said, heaving his chest in a sigh. "Attention up here, okay?"

I was startled back to reality. Since I had already disrupted class, without meaning to, I impulsively decided to ask a simple question that shot into my head, one that had been in the back of my mind for weeks.

"Okay, but really quick. Why do the kids call you Master Beyta?" I asked. It was a nickname I'd heard the kids use several times and I wanted to understand the context, not realizing at all that it was a sexual reference.

He stopped. He tilted his head. And he looked at me, blinking, for several seconds. I had no consciousness of having suddenly entered us both into delicate territory. I was aware that I was pushing it by asking a non-math question after interrupting the class already. But I wanted to know!

Master Beyta. Was he a black belt in karate? Was it a religious thing? A quick answer would satisfy my curiosity.

I could see the wheels turning as he calculated possible responses. Looking back, I realize he must've been assessing the sincerity behind my question (smart-ass or naive?), the answer to which would direct him down very different branches of a decision tree.

At the time, I was baffled that he was taking such a long time. *Just tell me,* I thought impatiently.

He didn't. In fact, he didn't say anything at all for a while. Instead, he slowly scanned the room, took another big breath, and said in an even voice, "Can somebody help Mary answer her question after class, please?"

Without skipping another beat, he turned back to the chalkboard and launched into the day's lesson.

I threw my hands up in a gesture of frustration, but once we moved on I completely forgot about it. And it seemed everyone else did too—no one mentioned it after class.

I went on after that year to a different high school than most of my friends, but I ran into a group of them when I was a senior. We hugged and said our hellos. One of them, who'd taken that class with me, suddenly burst out laughing.

"Oh my gosh, you guys wouldn't believe the time Mary asked Mr. Beyta, right in the middle of him teaching, why all the kids called him 'masturbate-a,' like it was nothing."

I winced. Wait . . . what? I said *what?*

Then the realization began to wash over me. *Oh, no. No, no.* The memory registered, I saw the whole scene unfold through a new pair of eyes, and everyone laughed as I shuddered in misery. I couldn't stop shaking my head.

Masturbate-a, not Master Beyta! *No, no, no.* I was nauseous. The other kids must've thought I was being mischievous in bringing up the nickname to his face. Oh my God. If he'd been triggered, he could've easily punished me, or leveled me with any number of sarcastic responses, exposing my naïveté.

I didn't even know I was in a minefield of possible humiliations that day, yet I made it out with my self-esteem intact. Mr. Beyta's grounded (and elegant!) response may not have been consciously oriented around empathy in that moment, but it was exactly the type of empathy in action my tender teenage soul needed.

—MARY GOYER, www.consciouscommunication.co

*Self-compassion is key because when we're able
to be gentle with ourselves in the midst of shame,
we're more likely to reach out, connect,
and experience empathy.*

—BRENÉ BROWN

Disdain From My Research Supervisor

After completing a doctoral program, I accepted a postdoctoral fellowship at Case Western Reserve University. By then, I had a certain lighthearted attitude toward life and research. I was to work on a research hypothesis that I had designed as a graduate student. I was very excited about the project. With good fortune, I was in a position to collaborate with a man who was both a skilled biochemist and an excellent researcher, and whose guidance I very much wanted.

Yet in one of our early conversations, he was so frustrated with me that he said: "Are you sure you have a PhD, Hema? You don't seem to be bright."

I felt sad and scared because I had been considered a good scientist and a productive researcher. My identity was suddenly in jeopardy. I felt like a failure since he was a renowned scientist; his words were the truth to me. It was a very painful experience.

After spending three hours crying and breathing, I returned to his office renewed with compassion. "Can I spend a few moments in your luminous presence so that I can brighten myself?" I asked.

By then, I think he was aware of his behavior, and he was very kind to me thereafter.

Particularly rewarding to me at that time was that I remembered to breathe. I understood that the best antidote to any violence was breathing. This has been one of the most exciting and major turning points in my development. By the end of the fellowship, we had published three papers together. My continued association with him has meant a great deal to me. After that day, my PhD stood for "psychologically healthy and delightful."

The time I spent breathing and crying was the time I allowed myself to stop and benefit from experiencing and reacting with freshness, taking time to remove any prejudice and restriction. This, to me, was meditation in its own form.

In those three hours of breathing, I became aware of the suffering caused by unmindful speech and inability to listen to others. I affirmed my own convictions to cultivate loving speech and deep listening in order to bring joy and happiness to my fellow beings and relieve them of their suffering whenever possible. After understanding that words can create happiness or suffering, I am now more conscious to learn ways to speak truthfully, with words that inspire self-confidence, joy, and hope.

—HEMA POKHARNA, www.journeysoflife.org

*We stay with empathy and allow others
the opportunity to fully express themselves
before we turn our attention to solutions
or requests for relief.*

—MARSHALL B. ROSENBERG, PhD

Saving Personnel During Budget Cuts

In many large organizations, teams and departments can "hire" other departments internally for work needed, or they can outsource the work. It all depends on the budgeting department, which acts as an intermediary as teams negotiate to work together rather than hire external help.

I was working with a senior executive who was in the process of bidding on an internal project to get his team hired. As the head of his department, he was focused on keeping the work within the organization rather than outsourcing it. He wanted to show what his team was capable of so they could further grow the company and, of course, so they could all remain employed.

It seemed as if his team had been hired, so they excitedly began planning the project until he found out the budget had been cut. The project was a no-go. He felt frustrated and disappointed because he had already planned on his team having the income as well as the work. And he was furious because he thought there was a personal issue behind the decision.

When he came to me for coaching, I listened to his story. He effortlessly set aside his frustration about office politics and was clear that his main priority was really quite simple: the budget. Would he have the funds to retain his staff?

With this focus, he knew he wanted a valid project to keep his team engaged so he wouldn't have to lay anyone off. We talked about his goal to keep his team employed, and what it meant for him to stand up for his team in terms of the company's values as a whole.

As we spoke, he was able to empathically connect with the person who controlled the budget, and how it must have felt for their integrity when they broke the news about the cut. He touched on the pressures that exist politically for the budgeting department, and he connected—at least mentally—with the person who made the top-down budgetary decision.

Once he had a chance to talk, without focusing on action steps, something fascinating came out of the conversation. Suddenly, two completely different strategies came to him, neither of which had occurred to him before. First, he wanted to approach the budget decision maker and listen empathically to make sure he really understood the constraints. And if there was room on their end to consider a creative solution, he had a renegotiation in mind.

When he had a chance to begin a conversation with the budget person, he said, "I understand you were asked to cut a certain amount from the overall budget, and that you did that by cutting from a number of different departments. Is that true?"

"Yes, that's it."

"And so you felt that you couldn't give us the money we'd hoped for, right?"

"Right."

"Okay, well, I have a completely different idea that would be good for the company and keep my team intact, and we would be working on something really important. Are you open to hearing it?"

His budgeting colleague seemed open to the idea and nodded.

"This company is committed to spending a certain amount of money on public service advocacy," he said. "I have a project in mind that would cost about X amount and is in line with our values." It was about the same as the amount of money cut from the team budget.

He then went on to outline an education-based outreach project in Africa that would focus on hygienic treatment of bottled milk products. He had the data on what it would involve and the number of lives saved. He wrapped up with more statistics to illustrate how the proposed project aligned with the company's social mission.

Ultimately, he made a connection and got the requested budget for the project approved. My client's team—all of it— had the resources they needed to work on something incredibly meaningful to them, far more satisfying than the original project would have been. And he restored the relationship with his colleague in the budgeting department.

He was so happy about the outcome. He said the situation would never have unfolded so well if he hadn't cleared his resentment to refocus on his core needs, which essentially boiled down to relationships and collaboration.

—DIAN KILLIAN, www.workcollaboratively.com

Being aware of feelings and needs,
people lose their desire to attack.

—MARSHALL B. ROSENBERG, PhD

A Dying Patient

In the late 1980s, I worked as a nurse in the hospice unit of a large hospital located in an area of Vancouver that had a substantial gay population. At that time, many gay men were dying of AIDS and it was painful for the whole community. I was caring for an AIDS patient, a young man who was close to death, when I learned what a simple yet profound difference it can make when I intend to listen with my heart.

This man was in his early thirties and only a few days away from dying. While he rested on the bed, his younger brother, who couldn't have been more than twenty-five years old, was standing on the other side of the bed watching everything I did.

He said, "Why aren't you starting an IV for him?" "Why aren't you tube feeding him?" He seemed so focused on everything I was doing, and every word out of his mouth sounded like an accusation.

I could have gotten defensive, but something magical happened in that moment. I can only describe it as a moment of grace.

I heard myself say, "This must be incredibly painful for you."

Instantly, his whole demeanor softened, his energy changed, and he began to cry.

I couldn't believe how pivotal that comment was. It changed our whole day together. It was easy for me to go there as soon as I could hear what was in his heart and in the words coming out of his mouth. That moment shifted his experience too, I believe. There was no longer a focus on why I wasn't doing this or that. I hope he was able to move through the grief he was facing with a little more grace and ease.

—ANNE WALTON, www.chooseconnection.com

Remember, empathy need not lead to sympathetically giving in to the other side's demands—knowing how someone feels does not mean agreeing with them.

—DANIEL GOLEMAN

Apologizing to My Students

I teach high school special education on an alternative campus, in a program designed to help students get back on track academically after excessive absences from school. It's not unusual for the kids I work with to suffer from anxiety and depression, so I've learned a lot about empathy and connection from these teens.

I remember one instance in which I was working with two girls who were upset with me, and I shocked them by doing something unusual from their perspective. I apologized.

I had initially asked them to be diligent and work on a math assignment for a set amount of time, which I assumed would be plenty of time to complete it. I essentially said, "Do your work, then you'll get some free time today."

When I checked back, they hadn't finished the work, so I took away that opportunity for free time. They were angry, and although I was confused about why they thought I was being unreasonable, I decided to have a chat with them to understand their perspective.

They thought I had asked them to stay busy and make

progress during the time frame; they didn't realize they were supposed to complete a specific set of work.

I took a breath. It can be frustrating to watch students not step up to what they are capable of accomplishing, and I needed a moment with my frustration.

I didn't change my mind about them losing their free time. But I did apologize for being unclear about my expectation. I said I wished I had been crystal clear in my directions during class so we could have started on the same page.

Neither of them said much, but I noticed their body language changed and softened when I acknowledged that we interpreted what I said differently.

After that, I asked, "Has an adult or teacher ever apologized to you for making a mistake?"

"No, never," they replied, clearly still surprised.

My apology was helpful in repairing the situation and I hope it conveyed that I care about their needs and perspectives, even if I hold a different point of view. Since that conversation, I've made a point to model for all my students how to handle making mistakes.

—KEVIN GOYER, www.consciouscommunication.co

*Skill at reading the currents that influence
the real decision makers depends on the ability
to empathize on an organizational level,
not just an interpersonal one.*

—DANIEL GOLEMAN

Honesty and Empathy With My Boss

J ayla saw the tip of the sun rising on the water. She wished she
could stop to take in the magic of the sunrise, but she was
cranky and tired. Deeper down she felt fear.

Three weeks earlier, she had left her job to begin a new job
in an elderly care facility. Days before beginning her new job,
three staff members quit, which doubled her workload. Although
she was earning the respect of her coworkers for handling
the workload well, she was exhausted. During the chaos and
exhaustion, she became ill and took two sick days to recover.

When she returned to the care facility, her morning was filled
with nonstop activity. Too tired to go downstairs and warm up
her lunch, Jayla laid her head on her desk. Two minutes later the
phone rang. It was Ursula, one of the nurses.

In a fast-paced Brooklyn accent, she said, "Jayla, I hope you're
settling in okay! I have to pick up my youngest who threw up at
school. Honey, one of the tasks of the job is that you carry out
home visits when a nurse is not available. We have one about
thirty minutes away and I need you to go. Get there before 4:00

p.m. this afternoon and you'll be fine. So sorry to spring this on you!"

Ugh. Jayla decided it had been a mistake to come to work.

While sitting in the cafeteria, a company coordinator named Tanisha stopped by to chat. She was livid when she heard about Ursula's call. "You shouldn't even be here," she said. "I get you want to be superwoman, but you've been superwoman for a couple weeks now. Ask one of the home aides from the other department if they can do the home visit."

Jayla looked away and shook her head. Tanisha softened her tone. "You might as well ask. Girl, it is not your job to sacrifice your well-being for this company."

Once she was back at her desk, Jayla took a moment to reflect. She wanted to carry out her responsibilities, but her body felt so heavy. Was it realistic to fear that her supervisor would fire her for asking someone else to do this task? She decided the priority was that clients get the support they need. It didn't matter who provided it.

Motivated by this logic, Jayla reached out to Juan, a home aide in another department, to see if he could do the visit for her.

In response, Juan said, "I wish I could help you out! I can't this time. It's good that you asked. We're human, right? I might be the one sick next time. Listen, I'll ask the other home aides I know and see if anyone is free, okay?"

Later, Juan texted, "I couldn't find anyone, sweetie."

Jayla was disappointed. She tried to connect with the situation: an elderly person in a neighboring town needed care. It was part of the commitment she made when accepting this job. With resolve, she got up, put on her coat, and headed out the door.

The visit went well. She arrived back home relieved, but so exhausted that she couldn't even brush her teeth. She slid in between her sheets and woke up when the alarm went off early the next morning.

Jayla met with her supervisor Rob. They seemed to be

developing a good relationship. Previously, Rob had apologized for the amount of work he assigned. He was also working incredibly long hours. Even though it was a hard time for both of them, she appreciated that they were bonding over the excess workload.

As the meeting wrapped up, Rob mentioned that he had heard about Juan searching for a substitute for her. He said, "Well, this job is stressful and sometimes you have to do things when you don't feel like it."

Jayla felt her body grow cold. She found herself nodding and saying, "Of course."

Later at her desk, she occupied her hands by tracing her micro braids. *Does he really think I'm lazy?* Jayla wondered. As she moved through the day, she thought of a hundred things other than "of course" that she could've said.

The following week, Rob made a similar comment. This time, Jayla felt sure that she needed to address it, but she wanted to do some prep first. His words rolled around her mind like a bad pop song on repeat. One evening, she took out her deck of Feelings and Needs cards. She looked through the Feelings cards, laying out the ones that resonated with her: Anxiety, Frustration, Numbness, Anger, and Fear.

As she looked through her Needs cards, she put Trust in the center. What would trust look like in this situation? Jayla twirled the Trust card between her fingers. *A supervisor who has my back. Knowing I would be respected if I said the workload was too much.* As she imagined the thoughts, her body relaxed.

Then she wondered what might be going on for Rob. He might be scared or worried. He probably also wanted trust and dependability in his employees. She thought about all the circumstances and pressures contributing to the situation.

She often witnessed an unhealthy dynamic where even though everyone was overworked, the everyday tensions of the job led some to point fingers at those who worked less, comparing sixty hours to their seventy. Jayla reminded herself that the bigger issue was too much work for too few people.

At the check-in meeting with her supervisor, Jayla planned to express her concerns to him directly. After exchanging pleasantries, she took a deep breath and launched in. "Rob, it's really important to me that we have a good working relationship. Is this a good time to discuss a concern I have?"

"Yes," he replied.

Jayla went on, "My intention here is to do my job fully. Feeling like we are a team helps me do that. I want to know that someone has my back if I'm not feeling my best. Since my job involves taking care of frail elderly people, I need to feel well for the sake of everyone's safety. I don't want to feel like I have to do everything on my own to be considered high-performing."

Rob nodded. "I'm happy you brought this up. You're probably feeling this because of something I said. I was really upset when I heard that one of the nurses asked you to do something and instead of taking care of it, you tried to figure out ways to have someone else do it." His body was tense, and his tone lost some of the softness that it had earlier.

Jayla wanted to defend herself. She paused to breathe, switching to empathy instead. "I'm guessing you probably wanted to know that you were supported when you heard that I asked for help for a job that is typically mine. You might have been worried and wondered if you could depend on me."

Rob's face changed. He didn't look as angry and seemed a little surprised. Jayla listened to her intuition to sit in silence for a few seconds as the words settled.

"This was an unusually hard month that we just had," she said. "I didn't realize I was so sick until I showed up for work. In fact, at lunch that day, I barely had the energy to go warm up my food."

His face looked pained. "I'm so sorry. I knew you were sick, but I didn't put two and two together."

"Thanks," Jayla said, ready to reassure him. "I'm fine and I'm sure it will be okay." Although it would have been easy to focus on her situation, Jayla really wanted Rob to get the sense that she understood where he was coming from and, more importantly, that she cared.

"I realize both of us are overworked. You're not supposed to get calls in the middle of the night or on weekends, but because we're short-staffed, you are getting those calls. I know you have kids. I imagine it's stressful and you want space to take care of yourself and your loved ones. Is that true?"

He nodded.

"I know you depend on my role so you can do your job. But because we've been short-staffed, you've been doing some of my duties in addition to yours. It's not fair to either of us."

He nodded. "It's a lot," he said, looking down.

Jayla continued, "I've worked for medical agencies before. I know they're typically short-staffed. It's not our fault this is a bad situation."

He nodded again in agreement.

"We all want to do a good job. Let's team up to deal with it," she said.

Naming the big picture released the remaining tension from the room. They warmly discussed the various items left on the agenda. She felt them become a team again, working toward building solutions.

At the end of the meeting, Rob said, "I feel so bad. I want you to be supported. It's just been really hard. I'll do better. Let me know what you need."

Jayla replied, "I get that you care about me and I really appreciate it." He nodded. With a smile, he walked off, and she knew that they were back in connection.

—PHOENIX SOLEIL, www.phoenixsoleil.org

Empathic connection has a very specific meaning and purpose. Empathy, of course, is a special kind of understanding. It's not an understanding of the head where we just mentally understand what another person says. It's something far deeper and more precious than that.

—MARSHALL ROSENBERG, PhD

Empathy in the Community

Caring for Strangers and Neighbors

The power of empathy comes alive in a special way when strangers and near-strangers connect with each other, sometimes under extraordinary circumstances. If it is our evolutionary programming to distrust anyone we don't know or perceive to be different from us, empathy gives us a way to plug in to each other's humanity and hold space for each other.

I've heard about school bullies becoming friends with their victims, thieves willingly paying reparations to those they've stolen from, and intrepid individuals fighting religious oppression with love—and doing so successfully. I've heard how empathy from a black female activist compelled a KKK leader to tear up his membership and join a civil rights organization. I've heard about cases in which imminent violence was averted because one person had the capacity to empathize with someone experiencing tragic levels of pain.

Roshi Joan Halifax, a Buddhist monk, says empathy is feeling resonance with someone else's subjective experience—somatic or emotional—and is required for compassion. Father Richard Rohr, a Catholic priest, agrees that empathy involves the capacity to connect to the suffering of other sentient beings and is an "integral part of spirituality."

Empathy for you might be a lived spiritual practice. It might be a tool for your social justice imperatives, enabling you to speak up on matters you care about in a way that doesn't alienate those listening. Or maybe empathy is simply about being a decent human being who cares about the dignity of others.

Whatever the case, I'm excited to share stories with you that may inspire more connection between you and strangers you meet every day. These stories illustrate how empathy can de-escalate conflicts, combat loneliness, and build human connection in the most unlikely places.

If we become skilled at giving ourselves empathy, we often experience in just a few seconds a natural release of energy that then enables us to be present with the other person.

—MARSHALL B. ROSENBERG, PhD

Going the Distance

As we crawled through Central London, I glanced up from my book and realized we'd passed the landmark Harrods store twice this wintry Sunday afternoon. Its hooded windows resembled a row of giant baby buggies, incandescent and full of delights for Christmas shoppers. Had the driver taken a wrong turn? Buses and cars were on all sides, and my mood darkened at the prospect of a long delay on what was already a three-hour journey home to the West Country.

Other passengers inside the dimly lit coach were no doubt having similar thoughts, but only one aired their views aloud. A thick, inebriated voice rose from the back seat, and I felt my mind tense into a ball of irritation tinged with anxiety. Here was a man needing someone to blame, and the driver who spoke with a heavy Polish accent would be his target.

Soon the man at the back of the coach had worked himself into a frenzy, threatening to punch this foreigner who didn't seem to know the route. Were his bellows reaching the driver? I wasn't sure, but every threat filled me with more dread. If he did assault the driver, the consequences could be serious for everyone on board. No longer able to focus on reading, and lacking headphones to create an insulated bubble, my fear and displeasure grew in equal measure.

I disliked the man's language. Like a needle stuck in seventies' vinyl, he intermittently spat the same curse: *cunt*. An old English word that once simply denoted female genitalia, it also has fascinating etymological links with underground water channels (*cundy*), knowledge (*kenning, cunning*), and power (*cunctipotence*). I had long crusaded to reclaim this misused word and its forgotten connections and literary usage (both Chaucer and Shakespeare loved using it in puns). But I hated what I judged to be this man's ignorance and misogyny.

In the seat across the aisle from me, a young woman jiggled her legs and glanced around, and I attributed her discomfort to the man's behavior. With the coach almost full, there was no option to move out of earshot. As this woman's senior, I wanted to intervene, to spare her this ugly tirade. But courage felt featherweight against my fear. What would happen if I spoke up? Might he redirect his vitriol at me?

The clock took forever to change, as if reluctant to display another minute passing. Our progress felt slower than I could ever recall on previous trips, probably because of the volume of Christmas shoppers. I shifted in my seat wondering what could be done.

Feeling as if there were a bird trapped beneath my rib cage, I finally turned and knelt up on my seat. Clearing the burr in my throat, I called out in the friendliest voice I could muster.

"Hey, mate. I can hear you're pretty annoyed about this journey taking so long. I know it's a real nuisance we're delayed."

Silence at first, and I wondered if he'd even heard. At last the man raised a bloated face and stared. Was that hostility in his slackened jaw? I managed a weakly encouraging smile.

"Yeah," he ventured. "Problem is that cunt of a driver doesn't know what he's doing!"

I swallowed, ignoring what felt like further provocation.

"Sounds as if, like me, you're feeling annoyed that the bus will be late getting back?" I was treading water.

He grunted an assent. Then added, "I wanna get to see my kids, but this foreign cunt's holding me up!"

My breath whistled as I exhaled, and I wondered if he'd caught that. Yet somehow the sound gave me courage to continue.

"Oh, I can understand it's important for you to see your kids this evening. No wonder you feel so upset!"

His face brightened, then took on a quizzical expression. "What do you do?" he inquired.

"What do I do for a living?" I checked, buying myself time. How should I respond? Despite being a professional writer and artist, I earn my living in various ways that feel meaningful and offer me the flexibility and freedom to pursue my creative practice. But I wasn't sure he'd understand. I needed the one bowstring to which he'd relate.

"I work with kids," I ventured. "I take groups out into the woods and teach them about nature, show them survival skills, that kind of thing."

"That's good," he replied, tapping the headrest in front of him with a tattooed hand.

"Thanks," I said. "I enjoy my work."

The man's features reshaped themselves, and I noticed a hint of sadness.

"I don't get to see my kids much . . . that's why this cunt's pissing me off!"

I nodded. "That must be hard for you, if you don't get to see your kids often and then you're delayed. No wonder you feel frustrated!"

He nodded, a smile pushing his cheeks toward his ears and revealing broken teeth. I could see he appreciated my empathy—but his cursing, with all its xenophobia and misogyny, was disturbing. Again, I felt protective of the younger woman nearby. I had to make a stand, and my inner bird was beating to be free.

"Listen," I said with the most charming tone I could muster. "I know this whole situation is making you angry, and there's nothing any of us can do about it. But I need you to know that every time you say the word *cunt*, it really upsets me, because it's like the most precious part of a woman's body is being used in a bad way. There's this young woman here," I added, gesturing in her direction, "and other ladies on the bus, and I'm sure none of us feel good about you talking like that. Would you mind stopping, please?"

At first, he stared, his mouth sagging visibly. As his head sank, revealing a crown lightly covered in black down, I caught his mumbled apology. After that he was quiet, and with a nascent sense of triumph I resumed my seat. The silence continued. At last, with relief washing through me, I picked up my book.

The next time I glanced out the window, we were crossing the flyover that takes traffic above rooftops of houses and shops westward out of London. Perhaps the driver's rerouting of our journey had been effective after all.

Half an hour later, the coach made its first stop at Heathrow Airport. Resuming a speedier rumble along the motorway, it stopped periodically in villages and towns, depositing passengers. As we approached the fifth stop, I was aware of movement behind me. The man was readying himself to leave. The interior lights went on and I lifted my head to say goodbye.

"Sorry for my rudeness earlier," he said in a gruff voice. "And thanks for telling me off. You gave me something to think about there!"

Astonished, I replied, "Well, thanks! And enjoy your time with your kids!"

As I watched him progress along the aisle, I noticed his tattooed fingers and knuckles gripping the backs of seats to steady himself, and various passengers eyed him as he passed. As he finally descended the steps, I felt our collective relief that the troublemaker was gone. We watched as the small, burly man in a studded leather jacket heaved his bag from below the bus and nodded at the driver who was helping an elderly woman with her suitcase.

As my attention returned to the inside of the bus, I became aware of people's faces, smiles, and appreciative nods in my direction. A smartly dressed older man approached with his hand extended to shake mine.

"Thank you so much. That was great what you did there!"

I received the compliment with a smile. Inwardly I acknowledged the Nonviolent Communication practice group I'd been attending for some time. While we often rehearsed various scenarios—like a bunch of amateur actors continually improvising and revising our lines—there was nothing like a real-life situation to prove I'd begun to acquire a skill.

—HELEN MOORE, www.natures-words.co.uk

> *The key ingredient of empathy is presence: we are wholly present with the other party and what they are experiencing. This quality of presence distinguishes empathy from either mental understanding or sympathy.*
>
> —MARSHALL B. ROSENBERG, PhD

Car, Clubs, and a Cab Driver

Back when I was living in Manhattan, I loaned my station wagon to a friend who needed it to move into her new apartment. We agreed that she would return it early that evening. I waited and waited, then waited some more. No call, no car. I drifted to sleep on my couch, still waiting.

At about two thirty in the morning, I was awakened by a phone call. "Thom, I just finished moving and I don't have the energy to return the car tonight."

"Where did you leave it?" I inquired.

She informed me that it was parked on a street in an unsafe part of town, with my golf clubs in plain sight in the back. Ten minutes later, after some serious self-empathy work (that's a story for another time), I headed out to rescue my car and my precious toys.

I staggered into the night and eventually found a cab. I climbed in and we headed along the edge of Manhattan Island down the West Side Highway. As we drove alongside the Hudson

River, we passed the USS Intrepid, a decommissioned battleship that functions as a floating museum.

From the back seat I could see only the cab driver's eyes reflected in the rearview mirror.

"The last time I saw that ship, I was stationed in Vietnam," he said.

We made eye contact in the mirror.

"That must bring up quite a bit for you."

"It does."

"EMPATHY NOTS"
Example

STORYTELLING

"My boss is worse than that."
"One time . . ."
"When I was in this situation . . ."

I listened into the silence that followed. More eye contact, more space. After a time, he spoke again.

"When we came back, everybody hated us."

We sat quietly as the tires thumped rhythmically on the seams of the road, sounding eerily like a beating heart. We just sat there, making space for his pain, his need to be seen, and for appreciation and love. I watched the pain slowly seep into his occasional glance.

"I imagine that was tough, risking your life like that," I said. "I bet it would have made a big difference to have gotten even *some* appreciation."

"Yes . . . yes, it would have."

Still seeing only his eyes in the mirror, I watched as the tears slowly filled his eyes. We continued our ride, without a word, and rolled through the empty streets to our destination.

A few minutes later we arrived. I reached through the little glass hatch and paid the fare . . . and with compassion and connection in my heart, I said a simple "thank you." I swung the door open and started on my way. From behind me, I heard the cab door opening. As I turned, there was my newfound friend, with an outstretched hand and a look of pure relief in his eyes, walking toward me. "Thank *you*." We shook hands and parted.

—THOM BOND, www.compassioncourse.org

*To listen is to lean in softly, with a willingness
to be changed by what we hear.*

—MARK NEPO

A Curbside Encounter

I drove up the road to drop off two greeting cards lying on the passenger seat beside me. I'd been there the day before to visit my dear friend and catch up on a decade of sharing. I had also visited with the rest of her family—a gentle husband, two daughters I'd watched grow into teenagers, and Harrison. He was their eldest child, a source of both pain and love.

Harrison was the catalyst for the cards that I'd addressed to my friend and her youngest daughter.

It had been a hard stretch for them. When we talked the day before, I heard exhaustion in my friend's voice, and I saw her eyes grow moist as she confided in me.

"Harrison's being *horrible* at the moment. He won't even talk to me. He's angry about his money paying for Erin's counseling."

Her look communicated the indignant thought, *It's because of him that she needs it.*

Of the three children, my heart opened particularly wide for Erin. She was the last to go under. One of the greeting cards beside me reached out to her, offering outings and remembering expeditions.

I pulled up outside their house and positioned the car over

a muddy verge. I posted the envelopes through the letter box before I noticed the sound of a vehicle behind me. I gestured to the driver that I was about to move, but apparently my hand signals confused him. He didn't seem to want to pass me, so he swung the car into the drive opposite my car to turn around. As the car stopped, I saw a young man get out of the passenger seat and lift an arm to wave goodbye. He turned and I realized it was Harrison.

He was old enough to be at university now, and I was still getting used to him having a semi-independent life. I waved and settled back into the driver's seat as he approached with his lopsided walk.

I lowered the windows, letting in fresh air and contemplating the irony of my encounter with the very person whose behavior was affecting the people I had written the cards for.

He leaned in and immediately I was held by the shining hazel of his irises. The corners of his eyes crinkled, alive with a genuine grin. Disheveled brown hair bounced on his head.

"Hello, you," I said.

A few sentences flowed about university and the impressive results he'd turned in. If this year went the same way, he would emerge with the equivalent of three good A levels and could sit for a degree if he wanted to.

His mum had shared the day before that the shift had been sudden—but welcome—when Harrison announced a few weeks earlier that he might like to go to university. His parents had not outlined any expectations because they wanted him to do whatever served him best and kept him and others safe.

We fell into companionable silence.

"And how's everything else?" I asked, inviting him to connect.

His lips fell into a line and his dark eyes were penetrating. He was deciding how to respond.

"Well, I'm not getting on that well with Mum at the moment." His voice was sad and tired.

"Uh-huh," I said, with a tone that I hoped communicated that I didn't mind whether he said more.

"It's just, well . . . I don't know if you know, but I get money because of my autism."

I nodded.

"Well, I asked her if I could have it and she said it was paying for Erin's counseling. And I don't think that's fair. I mean, I want Erin to have the counseling, it's not that. But I think it should come from somewhere else . . . It's *my money*."

"And you'd like to decide how it's spent?"

He nodded. "Yeah . . . I mean, I asked Mum where it goes, and she said it just goes in the general pot. I think that's selfish. I think she should be earning that money, not using mine."

I marveled for a moment at this radical assessment of worth, and the casual dismissal of more than sixteen years of full-on parenting.

I listened. He elaborated.

"I mean, Mum's doing this course instead of getting a job, but if she wanted to have children, then she should be working to earn the money we need."

It was the first time I'd heard his view on my friend's training course, and it was stronger than I'd imagined. I knew the vocation she was pursuing had been a source of some contention, but I hadn't heard that it was about economics.

"And Dad doesn't want her to do it." I watched as his face clouded. "I can't even look at her. I just keep remembering that moment when she slapped Dad's face and said, 'I hate you.' And he got in the car and drove away and didn't come back till very late."

There was fear in his face. And hurt. "I feel sorry for Dad," he said.

I kept eye contact and nodded. I wondered if he had said this to anyone else, but I also knew in that moment that it didn't matter at all.

I ventured a guess about my understanding of where this discussion had come to rest.

"I thought your mum wasn't thinking of a vicarage but maybe a chaplaincy, or something like that?" I suggested.

He paused. "Yeah . . . well."

A beat.

"You're still worried?" I asked.

"Mmm . . ."

I nodded again, my face solemn.

I breathed in and paused. We smiled ruefully at each other.

"Do you think you could tell your mum?" I asked.

"I don't know what to *say* to her."

His tone managed to hold both exasperation and acceptance. He seemed at peace with where they were. The strategy of disengagement was set to continue, because it was the best he could do to authentically manage where he found himself.

It made sense to me.

Then the curveball came.

"Do you think *you'll* have children?"

Twenty-five years of fearing that I wouldn't surged up my throat and hung at my lips. I paused, aware of a fork in the conversation, unsure which way to turn.

I could swallow everything back down, laugh, and deflect.

But here, now, it didn't seem balanced. I wanted to match his candor, respect his trust. I wondered if he could handle the honesty. Whether it would embarrass him or take him out of the connection he was enjoying.

He waited calmly, and I decided to risk it.

"Well, that's a big one."

He smiled gently, and, encouraged, I went on: "I've been going back and forth on that for years. For a while I thought I wouldn't be able to . . . and then, after we got married, well, things are complicated . . ."

I opened a door in my mind to the seven nieces and sole

nephew, in a place where girls are a financial burden and sons a family's security. I shut it again. Too much for today. My husband's family were minorities within a dominant culture and couldn't break free from their chains. The homes my nieces would marry into, when they reached that age, were likely to remain steeped in patriarchy.

"When we first got married, I wondered if we could, but other things happened." I remembered the births overseas, the new job, the maternity pay that wasn't available before two years of service, the ticking biological clock.

"And, I guess, now I worry that we're a bit old." This was also true and was the strand I could manage as his brown eyes held mine.

"I mean, if we had a baby tomorrow, by the time he was your age, and thinking about university, we'd be nearly seventy. I'm not sure that's fair."

He looked at me, his head to one side, warm and unruffled. Slightly surprised, but noticing, and stepping into, the trust.

"I'm not sure," he offered. "I think you'd be fit enough."

It's my turn to smile now. "Really? You think we could manage it?"

"Yeah, I don't know, somehow I've always thought of you as being able to do that."

Another pause, then he added, "You've got the right kind of energy."

A door opened again in my mind. It led somewhere else.

I felt touched and surprised. Ten minutes earlier, I'd been stopping off on my way home, to shove some cards through a letter box. The entire activity had been an afterthought conveniently tucked into the itinerary of my day.

Now something else had unfolded. Harrison walked into my afternoon and opened his heart, and then he opened mine.

I smiled at him.

"Thanks, Harrison."

He shifted his weight to the other leg. It was time to move. He was ready for something else.

I can't remember how we said goodbye.

I know he turned and walked up to the front door, feeling for a key in his pocket. I know I watched him, and briefly remembered the cards addressed to Harrison's mum and sister waiting on the mat. Then I glanced in the rearview mirror and pulled out from the curbside.

I knew we'd connected with each other. And over the days that followed, I wondered, *Do I have that energy?*

—LAURA HARVEY, www.sharedspace.org.uk

You listen with only one purpose:
to help him or her to empty his heart.

—THICH NHAT HANH

Immigration Checkpoint

It was 2015 and tensions were running high on the southern U.S. border. Hundreds of thousands of people were fleeing Central America in what had become an epic humanitarian crisis—people attempting to cross into the United States in hopes of finding safety, freedom, or economic well-being. That February, we took a family vacation to Honduras. On our return to the United States, we lined up to pass through U.S. Immigration and Customs, as usual. When it was our turn, my husband and I approached the agent as our travel-weary, eight-year-old daughter dawdled behind.

We said hello and handed over our three U.S. passports as the agent asked routinely, "Where are you coming from?"

"Honduras," my husband and I said at the same time.

"Family vacation," I added, preempting his next routine question.

The agent looked up at me. I offered a perfunctory smile in return. He looked at my husband, and I noticed the fine muscles around the agent's eyes contract ever so slightly.

By this time our daughter had meandered up to the counter and stood with us, sleepy-eyed and clutching her well-loved, black-and-no-longer-white stuffed kitty cat.

The agent took a deep breath and sat back, straighter and taller now. With no trace of a smile, he asked, "Is she your daughter?"

Disquieting thoughts flashed through my mind. *You're holding her passport and can see her photo and last name—so what's your question? Do you really think we'd come through the front door if we were up to something? Just what are you suggesting?*

Then it dawned on me that our family does not "match." We each have skin of different shades—peach, caramel, brown. My husband seems to fit a wide variety of profiles, and often gets pulled aside at airports for a pat-down and additional screening. Even back home in San Jose, he's been pulled over by the police twice while riding his bicycle in our neighborhood—"biking while brown," I call it. I've come to expect the disruption.

This time, though, it doesn't seem to be about him. Feeling both fierce, protective mama-bear energy and sweet tenderness for my sleepy little one, I replied, "Yes, she's our girl."

The agent's eyes darted from my face to my husband's, and back again. Slowly, he asked, "Is she from Guatemala?"

I told myself we had nothing to worry about; we had all the proper documentation—but my voice was thin.

"She was born in Guatemala."

His eyes narrowed. "I've seen a lot of kids from Guatemala. I recognize her features."

"We became a family through adoption."

He continued, "I used to work Border Patrol down in Texas."

Then I understood. My fears subsided and I beheld the person before me.

"Wow," I said. "That must've been a really tough job."

"It was," he said sadly, looking down.

"I can't imagine how heartbreaking that would be, every day, seeing people trying to escape desperate circumstances, willing to leave absolutely everything behind."

Softly and quietly, he added, "I had to turn back a lot of families. It was the hardest thing I've ever done."

We held each other's gazes and breathed together, taking in the weight of our brief exchange. He stamped our passports and said, "Welcome back to the United States."

—ANN OSBORNE

> *The behavior of others may be a stimulus*
> *for our feelings, but not the cause.*
>
> —MARSHALL B. ROSENBERG, PhD

Furious Neighbors

I walked out of my house and saw two men fighting. One looked visibly upset, then screamed and pretended to kick the other man's gray car. The car owner had his hands full with moving boxes and threatened to call the police.

I felt a bit anxious about the violence I was witnessing and even worried for my own safety while I watched the scene unfold. The man with the car was getting pretty frustrated, and I could sense his overwhelm. The first man, still ranting, spit on the gray car. But I sensed he was not really a threat to me. Just *angry*.

I walked right up to the man who was screaming and said loudly, "You look ANGRY!"

He then turned his attention to me, away from the gray car and its owner, and proceeded to tell me, loudly, how his pants got sprinkled when the driver drove past and splashed a puddle.

I continued by saying, "That must be frustrating!"

He began to walk away from the other man to tell me just how frustrating it was. As he spoke, I noticed he began to lower his voice.

The car owner looked at me with relief, and turned back to his moving boxes, happy to get out of dealing with an angry stranger.

As for the first man, I simply looked him in the eye and listened to his pain, while we slowly walked away together. I learned as he spoke that he was very poor, had just paid to wash his pants, and could not afford to wash his pants at the laundromat again. He totally calmed down as I listened, and when we got to his house he wished me a good day.

It was not easy, but I am glad I stopped to help these men. The situation could have spiraled out of control with the involvement of police, tickets, court dates, anger, and physical violence. I'm glad it didn't turn into a vicious cycle of pain.

—MANUELA SANTIAGO-TEIGELER

*True empathy is always free of any evaluative
or diagnostic quality. The recipient perceives
this with some surprise: "If I am not being judged,
perhaps I am not so evil or abnormal
as I have thought."*

—CARL ROGERS

Intensity and Diversity

As a trainee, I attended an intensive Nonviolent Communication workshop led by the late Dr. Marshall Rosenberg. Because there's a huge value around shared power and choice in Nonviolent Communication, our workshop strayed from the typical structure in which the leader is the expert whom everyone defers to. In our workshop, we established explicitly that everyone present in the room was responsible for creating the learning container, cultivating safety for each other, and expressing their own needs.

As a group, we had moved through the first phase of cautious hesitation. We felt pretty comfortable with each other and had reached that deeper level of community where self-disclosure, risk, and unguarded emotions really surface. It was during this deeper phase that a tense exchange happened one day. As it unfolded, I saw the power of empathy transform a conversation that might otherwise have resulted in the wreckage we often see when power and identity dynamics are at play, even in a room full of people gathering to learn about compassion.

As we began that morning, a Native American woman opened up about some stories of deep, deep chaos and heartbreak in her family and community. She spoke with increasing emotional intensity and graphic details of experiences that broke her heart. It wasn't the first time she'd shared with the group in this way. Since we arrived, she had repeatedly shared long stories of searing pain that took up a lot of space in the group. People tried to give her empathy, but it was unclear whether it resonated or made any difference.

There was pressure building in the room, and I think we all saw two options: suppress it and keep listening quietly, or express the frustration out loud.

Ten long minutes passed as we listened to one of the woman's stories, and then suddenly a priest in the group stood up, stomped his foot, and said, "Will you shut the eff up?"

There was shock and silence in the room, but I also felt a release. The woman was shocked into silence while he said a few more words. Marshall sat, watching this happen.

Then a second woman stood up and said to the priest, "How dare you attack her and slam her like that when she's trying to get help? That's the most inconsiderate, rude thing I've ever seen. How dare you?"

She was angry and blamed the priest, who now stood quietly.

Another young man, who was interested in social justice, jumped up and said, "Well, let's start with the priest because obviously he was feeling something strong. Let's hear from him. Don't shut him down. Don't do that."

I looked around the room at the four figures now standing— the woman who first spoke, the priest, the second woman, and the young man. Other hands were shooting up in the room. It looked like the exchange was turning into a big mess very quickly.

Marshall stepped in at this point and did three things. He asked the young man to pause, he acknowledged all the people who wanted to speak, and he noted the tension that was building in the room.

He asked the young man if he could say something. Marshall offered the young man an empathy guess along these lines, "Are you feeling a deep sense of frustration and maybe even some hopelessness as you speak, because you're wanting acknowledgment and people to express themselves fully and really be heard with acknowledgment? Is that it?"

The young man said, "Yes! That's what I'm trying to get, thank you."

Marshall replied, "I've got a little possibility for you. Would you be interested?"

When the young man nodded, Marshall said, "Might you want to guess about the woman who spoke before you, what her needs are, why she was speaking, and where the energy was coming from in her voice? Maybe guess her feelings and her needs?"

The young man nodded again and said, "Oh, okay. Yeah, I'm willing to try that."

He looked at the woman who had defended the first woman and asked if she was really scared when the priest stood up. Had it reminded her of her own family and now she really wanted to take a stand? He asked if it had taken a lot of courage for her to stand up.

As he spoke, we watched her calm immediately and visibly relax. He went on to ask if she really wanted to protect the first woman? To have safety, dignity, and inclusion for everybody?

Her eyes began to well up with tears as she nodded her head yes.

The whole group paused and watched as she processed waves of emotion after that acknowledgment. After several minutes, she took a breath and turned to the priest.

She said, "Listen, I'm sorry I yelled at you. I can see now that you were probably feeling frustrated because you wanted everyone to be able to participate. You wanted a deep sense of inclusion and understanding with everybody having space to express themselves. Is that it?"

The priest, who was now sitting, also began to relax and open up. He talked about where he worked and all the trauma he saw on a daily basis. He went into the workshop carrying a lot of heartbreak and said he couldn't take any more. He wanted relief and some help for that. So the group spent more time with his heartbreak and trauma, and although we spent just fifteen or so minutes listening to him, his grief began to shift. He felt like his needs were honored.

At this point, the priest turned to the Native American woman who had been so vocal about her struggles and apologized to her. He expressed regret about the effect he might have had on her.

She replied, "I'm touched but, well, it didn't bother me too much. I appreciate you standing up."

The dynamic in the whole room changed because of the empathy that flowed from one direction to the other. Just one drop of empathy from Marshall had reversed the escalating string of anger, frustration, and blame.

—TIMOTHY REGAN, www.rememberingconnection.com

Love chooses to believe the best about people. It gives them the benefit of the doubt. It refuses to fill in the unknowns with negative assumptions.

—STEPHEN KENDRICK

A Prisoner's Insight

I was running a class with a group of men in the San Quentin State Prison who were talking about one man's ongoing violent conflicts in the yard. The man said something about needing to "stand up for himself" to be respected.

An old-timer nodded and listened, then said to his classmate, "I'd do it differently."

"Okay, how?" the first man asked.

The old-timer replied, "I'd give the other guy the moment."

Fascinated, I jumped in and asked, "Wow, what's that? What does 'give him the moment' mean?"

"Well, when you see someone all twisted up, something's happened. He's not in his right state. Just back away, you know. Just give him the moment," he said.

"Oh," I said. "This is what I call empathy in action."

"What are you talking about?" several men asked.

To them, empathy was all about what you do or say. It hadn't occurred to them that *not* doing something could be a way to express empathy.

"It sounds like you've tried this but had a different name for it," I told them. "You've figured out by watching someone's body language and gestures when they're activated, that something's not working for them. So when you *gave them the moment* to just let them be without engaging, trying to correct, or anything else . . . that was empathy. Giving him the moment was empathy."

That day, they learned that empathy doesn't need to be about words at all. And I was reminded just how much better the world would be if we all had the space to *give someone the moment* more often.

—MAIR ALIGHT, www.mairalight.com

If your compassion does not include yourself,
it is incomplete.

—JACK KORNFIELD

Self-Loathing to Self-Acceptance

At a four-day healing seminar, a fellow participant had paid for a session of intensive personal work supported by the whole group. I offered to record it with my phone, so she wouldn't have to worry about taking notes. I was really happy to contribute in this way because her session was quite involved, lasting at least an hour. I figured she'd be glad to have a recording to reference later.

After the process ended and I was satisfied that I'd captured a lot of valuable work for her, I looked at the screen and saw the word *Done*. So I hit the little red button—which swiftly erased the entire recording.

In denial, I grabbed a techie friend and asked, "Okay, now what did I do wrong with this recording?"

She replied, "Well, there's no recording here."

"No, no, no!" I said. "I must have done something wrong. It must be saved somewhere. I could not have possibly done that."

She looked again and repeated, "There's no recording here. I'm sorry."

I was in shock and felt my stomach tighten. My chest clenched and a heavy sensation of shame poured over me, like a can of paint dumped over my head.

Before I knew it, familiar thoughts circled in. *How could you have done this? You know you're no good at this stuff. How could you let this happen? Why didn't you just ask somebody else to help you?* These self-berating phrases wouldn't stop. As it dawned on me that the recording had definitely been erased, I cried in spite of myself.

Another participant, Maria, saw my tears and asked if I'd like support. I was still in shock and denial, with grief and shame mixed in. She spoke in a calm tone, which helped me breathe.

"Are you kind of panicked?"

"Yeah, I am," I replied. "My throat is all closed up and my body is shaking."

"And scared?"

"Kind of! I'm feeling scared because I can't believe that I did that, that I could blow it so badly."

My friend had paid a pretty penny for her work. The process was complicated enough that everyone who had done a session had taken pages of notes for themselves. Otherwise, the important details could slip away like a dream upon awakening.

Maria asked, "Did you really want to be helpful?"

"Yes!" It seemed obvious. *Of course I'm upset! Of course I feel shame. I'm crying!*

Despite my frustration, it was better than sitting alone in self-criticism. Her company was good, but my shame continued to spiral. Maria sat through all of it, listening and sometimes asking more questions. What else was up for me? What else was I needing? *Oh, so many things. To be competent in technology, to contribute, to see myself as someone who had confidence in figuring things out in the future.*

The negative voices inside were deafening. *You'll never be able to do something like this again. You can't be trusted.* All of the old childhood blaming and self-shaming were right there. But my body had relaxed some.

Then I noticed my friend, the woman I'd let down, was sitting close by. She didn't know about what happened, and I realized I had to confess right away.

I grabbed a chair next to her, crying still, and said, "Oh my God, I can't believe what I just did. It was so important to me to make this recording for you and it didn't work. It didn't happen. I recorded over it and I'm just so sorry."

I could barely talk, I was crying so hard. She just looked at me with so much love in her eyes.

"Oh well," she said. "Those things happen."

I couldn't believe it. She didn't get what a horrible, awful thing I'd done. She didn't understand how badly I'd screwed up. She was so loving and . . . unconcerned! I was stunned.

She said, "Actually, what's really moving to me is how much you care, how important this was to you."

We talked a bit more and hugged. After I had a chance to recover, I noticed something pretty incredible. The earlier shame, only some of which was related to the incident itself, had drifted away. I kept opening the closet of my mind, expecting to find the ghosts and skeletons . . . but they were gone. No perseverating for weeks. Nothing. Those self-criticisms just left. For me, receiving my friend's empathy was like relaxing on a lounge chair under an umbrella on a tropical beach, listening to the gentle sound of ocean waves.

—KATHERINE REVOIR, www.richerliving.org

The hearing that is only in the ears is one thing.
The hearing of the understanding is another.
But the hearing of the spirit is not limited to
any one faculty, to the ear, or to the mind.

—CHUANG TZU

Meeting Honey

I had just accepted a position as the new doctor in a small New England town. A short time after I started, while I was still focused on getting to know my patients, a woman named Roberta came to see me. She said she was having trouble sleeping. I did my normal assessment to get a grasp of things when she told me that her partner, Honey, had died two years previously. It was the anniversary week of Honey's death.

"Oh, my goodness, you lost your partner just two years ago? And we're on the anniversary right now?"

"Yeah."

"Oh, that sounds painful!"

"Yeah," she replied. "We'd been together for fifteen years. We were a perfect fit."

"Oh, wow. So things worked really beautifully in your partnership, huh?"

"Really beautifully. I was so well met by Honey." She began to tear up. "I have a hard time imagining there will ever be another love like Honey's in my life."

"That must be so hard for you!" I said. "I really hear how much you miss her. And that you wonder about whether you'll have that depth of love again."

"Exactly." She sighed, shoulders dropping.

We sat together in silence for a long moment, after which she shifted back to her issue of sleep.

"Sleep really has been rough. It's hardest at night."

"Mmm, without Honey, you can't sleep."

"Right."

"Yeah, I'm really getting that," I said. "This has had a big impact on you in all sorts of ways, it sounds like."

"It has," she acknowledged.

"Okay. Well, let me ask a question. What kind of support do you have?" I asked.

"Well, lots of support in a way. I'm actually very lucky. I have a few friends who really get it, but I'm trying not to burden them. And the tired part? I'm exhausted and there's nothing they can do about that."

"EMPATHY NOTS"
Example

SPIRITUALIZING

"It's in God's hands."
"It was meant to be."

"Got it. Your friends are understanding, but it sounds like you're wanting to be conscientious of their bandwidth for all you've got going on. Is that it?"

"That's it."

"And you're really struggling with the sleep thing this week, which brought you here."

"Yeah," she replied. "I haven't slept in the past two years."

"Right, you did say that. I think you said it's been hard at night all along. You haven't settled into a sleep routine that works for you since Honey passed."

"Yeah."

"Okay, and I'm wondering, do you have a sense of what you need? What you were hoping to have happen today?"

With that, we shifted back into consult-mode and went through some options to help with sleep. We discussed medications and the various other things she could do to make a difference with the quality of her rest.

Before Roberta went on her way, she thanked me, deeply, for the help.

"Oh, wow." I responded. "So our talking really offered some support. I'm glad. And thank you so much for being willing to share what's in your heart with me."

We hugged goodbye, both touched by our time together.

About two days later, another new patient came in. Judith was brand new to me as well, so I sat down to learn about who she was and what brought her in. She said she was experiencing terrible grief. Her dear friend, Honey, had died and it was the second anniversary of her death. They were both artists, had collaborated on all sorts of projects, and had been longtime family friends.

Judith said Honey was fun and bright and vibrant and lively. She didn't quite know what to do with the grief she still felt or how to be supportive to Honey's partner. Not to mention her own partner, who had been Honey's best friend. She said everyone was just reeling for months after Honey's transition. So we spent time in connection around Judith's terrible pain, which she was trying to keep from affecting her loved ones.

A day later, I met Jane. Jane came in to see me because of terrible anxiety, saying that her best friend, Honey, had died two years ago. I realized Jane was one of the people Judith mentioned.

I sat in shock as I listened to Jane say how she and Honey used to walk together on the beach every morning, early-early, as close confidants. She and Honey shared both clothing and a special sense of humor. Jane was having a particularly hard time because it was coming up on the second anniversary of Honey's departure and life just wasn't the same without her.

So I got to know Roberta, Judith, and Jane all in the same week because they needed a doctor for their insomnia, grief, and anxiety. Of course, I couldn't let them know I had talked to all of them about Honey or that they were having a shared experience of pain. In terms of privacy, I couldn't reveal the story that unfolded to anyone. It had to be enough that I got to know Honey through each of them. And there was something beautiful about that, really. There was a certain aesthetic to the empathic way I worked with each of these women, their stories of Honey, and their symptoms, all while upholding the silence of confidentiality.

I also found it remarkable that all three women went to such an intimate place with me, which was in part a desire to spare the others. They opened up to me—a person they had never met— about what was really going on, while at the same time missing in each other what they all seemed to long for deeply.

Later, because it was a small town, I became part of their worlds as more than a doctor. As their friend, they invited me to a beach party. During the party it became evident to all three that they'd told me about Honey within days of each other.

I think it was Jane who tipped off the realization, when she said how much better she'd felt since we met around the anniversary of Honey's death.

Roberta, shocked, turned to me and said, "I went to see you when it was the anniversary of Honey's death!"

"Get out of here! I did too!" chimed in Judith.

I was finally able to acknowledge it. "Yes. I met all of you because of Honey. And through each of you, I also know Honey, which is really beautiful."

The four of us connected deeply while I lived there. At different points, they would say things like, "You're so much like Honey! Wow, you even look like her! You and Honey are surprisingly alike."

How interesting to know a woman, no longer with us, through the eyes of others who loved her. That's a legacy of connection I'm touched to be a part of.

—MARGARET GOLD

When we settle our attention on
other people's feelings and needs,
we experience our common humanity.

—MARSHALL B. ROSENBERG, PhD

Was I Being Attacked?

After inquiring about a spiritual practice group I was interested in, I attended two meetings with key members to get a sense of whether I was a good match for the community. During the first gathering, I felt uncomfortable around one of the women, Dee.

Dee rarely smiled with the rest of us, and as she shared her background stories, I felt that she did so in a competitive way. As she recounted one particular memory, I felt a surge of aggressive energy pulse toward me. I threw up a protective circle to deflect her energy, but this experience felt like a warning flag. I didn't want to navigate safety issues in a spiritual practice group. I wanted to focus my attention on staying open to Spirit.

I left the meeting feeling a little worried.

At the next gathering, Dee and I sat on the same couch. As the group began chatting, she turned sideways and stretched out her leg until her toe was about two inches away from me. Minutes later, she moved again, this time nearly touching me. I felt intruded upon. I took her actions as a disregard and disrespect for my space.

"Assault" is legally defined as when someone enters another's personal space, and "assault and battery" is defined as someone entering another's personal space and touching them, usually with violence. As an incest survivor, I pay close attention to my day-to-day boundaries. I use this information to decide whether I want to receive hugs from others, for example, and I'm pretty comfortable letting folks know when I feel open to being touched and when I don't.

In this case, I realized my sense of trust and ease were amiss, so I decided to speak with Dee about it.

Before speaking with her, I recognized that my ideas about her being "aggressive," "intrusive," and "disrespectful" all needed examination. Thinking through what I wanted when I had those judgments helped me calm down a little. I felt much more settled after translating these thoughts into how much I liked care, safety, and mutual respect.

Next, I began to wonder about Dee's motives during these interactions. I knew she had experience in theater and wondered if, perhaps, the energy surge I felt in our first meeting was her theatrical charisma projecting into the room. I also knew her job involved leading big groups, so maybe she had a habit of taking charge. When she stretched her leg on the couch, perhaps she was being friendly without checking to see if the gesture was received that way.

There was enough uncertainty that I wanted to check things out with her. As neutrally as possible, I described to her what had happened and the concerns I had.

"The first time we met, you were speaking about a particular experience and I noticed a surge of energy from your direction. I feel confused and want to understand what was going on for you at the time. Were you aware of this energy during our first meeting?"

"No," she replied. "I didn't realize that happened. I do know, however, that when I feel passionate about something, my energy can get pretty big. I've heard that before."

"Oh, okay, so hearing something about your big energy isn't entirely new for you."

On one hand, that was a relief to hear, because it meant that what I initially interpreted as aggression was something else. On the other hand, I wasn't sure if I could trust that I would feel safe if she was unaware of how she pushed energy out into the room.

"When I hear about your big energy, I feel torn. There's relief knowing I'm okay in terms of safety. At the same time, I feel unsettled because I'm new in the group and want to relax into our spiritual work without distraction. If you feel excited, would you send your energy away from me?"

She thought for about fifteen seconds before answering, "Yes, I can do that."

After a few breaths, I continued, "Okay, well let me check in about something else."

I described how she almost touched me on the couch. I tried to stay neutral as I asked, simply, if something was going on for her—rather than make any assumptions about her intentions.

"Yeah!" she replied, with a shudder. "The day we shared the couch, a chronic pain in my hip suddenly got worse. Sometimes it can just stab at me, so I was stretching to prevent a painful muscle spasm."

"Oh, got it. So you were focused on taking care of your hip, huh?"

"Exactly, yes."

I felt a little calmer hearing what was going on for her, definitely not wanting anyone to tumble into serious pain if it could be prevented.

"That makes total sense; I really do get that. So here's the thing for me. I've been through some painful experiences as a child. I am an incest survivor. Boundaries and safety are, as you might imagine, really important to me. So when we had these few moments where I felt uncertain about my safety, it raised some concerns for me about working in circle with you in this group."

"I don't see how me stretching was about safety," she said, with a little charge that made me feel like she might be upset.

"When people come inside my personal space, which for me

is about four inches away, my panic warning bells go off, shouting 'Am I safe?! Is it safe?!'"

"I didn't know all that was happening for you when I stretched out my leg. Were you worried?" she asked.

"I sure was," I said. "I'm relieved to understand what was going on for you. Would it help if I let you know when I have a concern in a specific moment instead of waiting until later to talk about it?"

"That would help," she said with a smile, "because I was worried we'd have to take a lot of time processing stuff. My life is so busy and I don't want to spend time outside of the circle going over stuff later. I also don't want to walk around on eggshells when I'm in the group."

"No, I wouldn't want that for either of us," I responded.

"How we can handle these different sensitivities between us?" she asked.

"I think talking about things right away can help, especially if we both assume goodwill for each other."

When I asked if she had any requests, she agreed to ask me if she is ever unclear about my comfort related to touching. In turn, I agreed to attend a couple more meetings to be sure I could work in the presence of her energy.

"I'm grateful you decided to speak with me about what was going on for you," she said. "I would feel disappointed if you just left without checking out my side."

We decided to play things by ear, and to check in as needed. Earlier in my life, I would have walked away from this group, awash in resentment and distrust, assuming Dee had ill will toward me. I would have missed out on a potentially amazing opportunity. Looking for the needs that Dee and I both had made our difficult conversation navigable instead of impossible. My increased understanding led to more hope and, ultimately, a deeper sense of connection with her.

—MEGANWIND EOYANG, www.baynvc.org

Animals are the bridge between us and
the beauty of all that is natural.

—TRISHA MCCAGH

In Search of Perfection

When I first went to India, I fell in love with the beautiful, hand-embroidered Kashmiri shawls. I was enamored of the exquisite handiwork and painstaking details in the colors, patterns, and fine stitchwork. I was determined to buy one for myself.

At the Kashmir Emporium, I stepped up to the counter and asked to see some shawls of a certain color. The clerk pulled out a single shawl and placed it on the counter, as if his job was done.

The shawl was nice, but I was looking for something else.

"May I please see a few higher-quality ones?" I asked politely.

He pulled out some others—lovely, but still not quite what I had in mind. This went on for several rounds.

Finally, I said, "Thank you, these are all very beautiful. Now, please show me several of your finest."

He cocked his head and looked at me closely, sizing me up.

He reached under the counter and pulled out a shawl enclosed in a clear, protective wrap. With a flick of the wrist, he tossed it onto the glass countertop. It spun around on the smooth glass before coming to rest in front of me. I felt the soft cashmere and examined both sides of the finely embroidered border.

Stunning, I thought, this time really lingering to appreciate the incredible patience and technical skill it took to create a work of such beauty.

I knew we were close. "I'd like to see one more," I said.

He paused, then reached into the wooden cupboard behind him and brought out the *pièce de résistance*—the one that truly took my breath away.

This was it. A cashmere shawl with a dense, four-inch silk border and stitches impossibly minute. The fine-needle embroidery was so intricate and well executed that the two sides of the shawl were nearly indistinguishable. Sheer beauty.

"It takes the artist more than two years to complete one of these," he said with great pride.

It was exquisitely beautiful, absolutely flawless, and utterly perfect. I couldn't really afford it but I bought it anyway.

Back in San Francisco, a dear friend came by one evening to see some textiles I'd picked up in my travels. At the end of the evening, I left the stack of treasures on my bench, where they remained for several weeks.

Weeks later, while tidying up, I saw my prize Kashmiri shawl at the bottom of the stack. I had a sudden, sinking feeling. Lifting it to the light I saw, to my horror, tiny specks of light shining through the finely woven threads like stars in the night sky. Moth holes. Damned moth holes.

I remembered how my mother had taught me to take good care of my precious things. When I was a kid, the pungent scent of mothballs filled my mother's storage closet, protecting our family's fine woolens and silks. I learned then that moths are dreaded pests to be feared and guarded against.

Filled with rage and shame, I chided myself: *How could you have been so careless? What were you thinking?*

Clearly, you weren't thinking, I responded with disdain. I tried to console myself. I tried to rationalize the situation, telling myself it wasn't so bad, that I could get the shawl rewoven.

I should have known better. I agonized about it, over and over—and over—again.

Some years later, I discovered something that took me completely by surprise: It's not the adult moths who eat holes in fabric. Rather, the adult females lay their eggs in the most hospitable environment they can find, so when their larvae hatch, the new baby moths have something nourishing and easily digestible to feed on.

As this piece of information sank in, I thought about my precious shawl. *Was it for real? A hideous moth did not chomp holes in my precious cloth, but rather laid her delicate eggs there?*

I felt a wave of wonder for the mama moth that has instincts, just like mine, to nurture and protect her young. That mama moth wanted the safest, softest bed for her child. And she wanted her baby's first food to be the tastiest, most easily digestible she could find. I wanted those things for my baby too.

All along, I had been demonizing these big, ugly creatures, cursing them for ruining my perfect shawl.

Now, my shawl is more beautiful than ever to me. I see each tiny hole as a call to connect with the web of life and remember my wild, instinctual self—and to bring sweet compassion to my own, perfectly human flaws.

—ANN OSBORNE

The more we empathize with the other party,
the safer we feel.

—MARSHALL B. ROSENBERG, PhD

Heckling Baseball Fans

Going to a baseball game was not my first choice for a Saturday activity. Despite my misgivings, however, I found that I was enjoying myself . . . until about a quarter of the way through the game when a group of guys came in. They were shouting obscenities at the players, which was really hard for me to hear.

"What a fag!" "Get some balls!" "You fucking suck, Smith!"

You get the idea.

The guys laughed and egged each other on, but just one of them was doing most of the shouting.

Their comments were so painful and disturbing to me that I told my boyfriend I might want to leave. But then I thought, *Maybe I could talk to them and ask them to stop making those obscene and offensive comments.*

A lot of fear came up in me as I had this thought. I sat with it for a while, took a few breaths, and gathered my courage. I went over to have a talk with them.

I walked right up to the guy who was the noisiest, offered my hand to shake, and said, "Hi, I'm Becka."

First, he looked confused, then proud. He puffed his chest out, glanced around at the other guys, and faced me again with a charming smile. I'm pretty sure he thought I was hitting on him.

I hadn't figured out what to say yet, so I began by asking how he was and whether he was enjoying the game. Then I got to the point.

"I came over because I heard you guys shouting things to the players out there and I'm curious about it. Why do you do that?"

"Oh, they don't mind," he said. "This is how it always is. It encourages them. We always do this to each other."

It turns out he was shouting comments to people he knew and regularly played games with.

"Oh, so this is how you guys connect and kind of show your support for each other?" I asked.

"Yeah."

"Wow, that's so interesting. You know, when I heard your comments, that's not what I thought. I thought you hated them! If I were out there hearing that stuff coming my way, I would be hurt. It would be hard to even hear those things."

He said, "Ah, yeah, well you're probably just sensitive. We can handle it. We always do this with each other."

At this point, I realized I didn't need them to stop making comments. My intention had shifted away from trying to change their behavior toward wanting to understand their perspective. My body loosened as I let go of my judgment and agenda. Instead I felt open and curious. I still disagreed with their choice of words to motivate their teammates, but I let go of labeling them "wrong" or "bad" people.

I felt a sense of satisfaction for being brave enough to talk and connect with them. That seemed like a big enough accomplishment for one day.

After I walked away, they stayed quiet—they stopped heckling on their own! Shortly after that, they left the stands.

I don't know if they left because of me, but I'm proud of the courage and vulnerability I practiced that day. I was able to connect and develop some understanding with a group of people

I had vilified. It was an empowering and compassion-building experience that has continued to stay with me.

—BECKA KELLEY

The ability to offer empathy to people in stressful situations can defuse potential violence.

—MARSHALL B. ROSENBERG, PhD

Antidote to Road Rage

One Saturday, I was driving home along a busy two-lane highway in Arizona when a motorcycle pulled onto the road directly in from me. It was a dirt bike and the rider was dressed in full racing leathers and a helmet. He was driving well below the speed limit and I came up behind him and followed him toward town. Suddenly, he slowed down to a crawl, traveling about five miles an hour, so I did too.

Meanwhile, the traffic backed up a long way behind me. As we approached the first traffic light entering the town, the motorcyclist pulled over. As I drove by to pass, he pulled up behind me and began following me—closely and purposefully.

I thought he might be angry at me, perhaps for following him more closely than he liked, and I didn't know what he might do. I was worried and afraid to pull over because of the potential for violence. I decided to stop near a lot of people, hoping that having witnesses might change the context of our encounter.

I stopped and the motorcyclist jumped off his bike and approached my car. As I rolled the window down, he began yelling at me and threatening to pull me out of the car and beat me. I was terrified.

I took a breath, and spoke energetically: "I get it, you're really mad. You want to be safe out there on the road."

He stopped in his tracks and took a step back. The words clearly touched him. He wasn't expecting to be heard. At that moment, the entire situation shifted.

"That's right. I do want to be safe," he said.

He took another moment to tell me his thoughts and then left. No fists were thrown and as I watched him drive away, I breathed a huge sigh of relief. Genuine empathy is a powerful thing.

—MARK SCHULTZ, www.nvctraining.com

Empathy is like riding on a wave;
it's about getting in touch with a certain energy.
But the energy is a divine energy that's alive
in every person, at every moment.

—MARSHALL B. ROSENBERG, PhD

Empathy in the Face of Power

I was heading to a holiday party I'd organized with a bunch of supplies in tow. I was taking the subway, something I often did as a New York City resident, with all the decorations and food packed in a large cart with wheels to make it easy to transport.

By the time I got to the subway, I was running late and in a hurry. I couldn't fit through the turnstile with my cart, so I decided to see if I could open the service gate with my MetroCard. In the past when I needed to use the gate, I had gotten the attendant's attention first before swiping, and then waited for them to open it. I never knew for sure if that was necessary, since there was a swipe machine next to the service gate. Swipe cards were still relatively new and the whole gate process was a bit of a mystery to me.

Because I was running late, and the attendant was busy with other customers, I decided to try it. I swiped my card and the service gate opened! I went through. Success! How exciting—I told myself I'd never bother getting the attendant's help again if I needed to use the gate. I was so pleased!

Suddenly, a police officer stopped me.

"You didn't pay," he said, gesturing toward the gate.

I was confused. "Didn't you see me swipe my card?" He was standing there when I swiped my card and the gate opened.

"Yes," he said, "but it doesn't matter. You don't have a service entry card, so the scanner would not have read your card."

I'd entered the subway system illegally. As I absorbed his words, he repeated himself.

"You got in without paying. The gate swipe machine only reads service entry cards."

It made no difference to him that the gate opened when I swiped my card. He said it was already unlocked. *Now, how could I have known that?* I wondered. I assumed the card worked.

"Ignorance of the law is no excuse," he maintained.

Flustered, I wanted him to trust my intention and acknowledge that I'd meant to pay. He had already written the ticket, though, so there was no point in further discussion.

I told the officer I was planning to go to the hearing and I asked him if he'd give me his word that he'd also attend. It wasn't so much about the ticket or fine. Being cited bothered me on principle and I wanted to be heard. The officer looked surprised because he knew I'd automatically win the case if he didn't show up, but he agreed. We'd see each other again in six weeks.

Before my court date, I did a number of things to get ready. Consistent with the Nonviolent Communication concept of having a clear observation, I took some photos of the gate to demonstrate the lack of signage to indicate it was for service entry cardholders only. I also prepared myself by journaling, getting lots of empathy, and practicing role-plays with my empathy buddies. I knew that sitting in front of two authority figures—a judge and an officer— would be challenging and triggering for me.

Because of their structural power, I assumed they would follow the letter of the law and bureaucratic protocol. I wanted to ready myself in a way that was different from my earlier patterns of showing up to authority with passivity or defiance. I wanted to handle it from a place of choice, empowerment, and conviction. In all of my self-prep, I had gotten clear on my core needs, which relaxed and calmed me.

On the day of the hearing, I was on edge but relieved that our meeting was in a modest office, not a courtroom. The police officer showed up and sat beside me. The setup reminded me of a mediation; the officer and I were on the same side of the table.

The judge read the complaint and asked the officer to give his version of events. He kept things simple and factual: the date, time, location, and that he'd observed me entering without paying.

Then it was my chance to speak.

I faced the officer and said, "I think I understand your point of view. At the most basic factual level, I did enter the system without paying. And for you, the intention isn't as important as the reality. I skipped paying—unbeknownst to myself—and even though the gate opened as I used my card, it's still my responsibility to know the law. The rest, at a certain level, doesn't matter. Is that right?"

He gave a nod of acknowledgment.

I continued, "I'm imagining it would be hard for you to do your job any other way."

I checked with him again, and he nodded.

I moved on to share what really mattered to me about this situation.

"I'm curious and confused. You were standing there when I swiped and went through the gate. Do you think I could see you standing there?"

"Yes, I imagine you could," he replied.

"And did you notice how surprised I was when you stopped me?"

"Yeah, you did seem surprised."

I showed the judge my photographs.

"While ignorance of the law is not an excuse, I think it's clear that my intention was to pay. After I went through the gate, I had no reason to believe that I hadn't paid, because the gate opened after I swiped."

I paused for a moment and took a breath. They were both with me, and I felt relatively calm and collected as I talked, even though that tinge of nervousness wasn't completely gone.

"Here's the thing. I hear your perspective . . . ," I said, with a breath for composure as I glanced at the officer. "And I'm really wanting some understanding, shared reality, and trust here. Even in a city the size of New York, I would love for there to be some trust about people's intentions. Some benefit of the doubt, you know?"

The judge took a moment to study the photos of the gate. She also seemed moved by hearing my core desires of living in a city where there is human trust and connection.

"I get what you're saying," she replied.

"I mean, how else can we live together and operate in a city of this size? I know this conversation started because of not paying a fare, but I invite you both to consider the meta-view of how we live and relate to each other. That's what I'd like, more than anything else."

"Okay," said the judge. "I can appreciate your point. Thanks. Let me think about it."

When she gave her decision, the officer was clearly surprised, even taken aback. The judge seemed a little surprised herself.

"This is the first time I've made a ruling of this kind to overturn a ticket like this."

She went on to say that she needed a few minutes to talk with her supervisor, otherwise he wouldn't understand her decision when he saw it. While we waited, I thanked the officer for honoring his agreement and coming to the hearing. I appreciated him giving me an opportunity to be heard. If he hadn't turned up, I would have won the case automatically. But I had deeper needs: to be seen for my intentions, and to be heard for my vision of the kind of place I want to live in.

That day, in that hearing, I had an opportunity to live in the type of city that I envisioned, where intentions, trust, and human connection matter. About five months later, I noticed the service gates were clearly marked: "Service Entry Cards Only." And the picture of the regular MetroCard, which had confused me in the first place, was gone.

—DIAN KILLIAN, www.workcollaboratively.com

Peace requires something far more difficult than revenge or merely turning the other cheek; it requires empathizing with the fears and unmet needs that provide the impetus for people to attack each other.

—MARSHALL B. ROSENBERG, PhD

Surviving at Gunpoint

I was invited to be a supporter in the kitchen at a four-day Lakota Sun Dance in Chacon, New Mexico. At the time, I was living a simple life, as a wandering spiritual seeker, possessing only what could be carried on my own back.

I had no car, so I waited on the side of the road to get a ride from one of the town neighbors to go to the dance in the very rural village in Mora County, the poorest county in the United States.

Rain was coming down hard, so I sang songs to the Beloved Divine Energy of the Universe while I waited, to persist in my practice of Thinking Restoratively to See Restoratively.

After I sang prayerfully for about twenty-five minutes, a man stopped to pick me up. To avoid getting further soaked by the downpour, I jumped in the cab of the truck and set my bags on the floor.

He asked me where I was going.

"Chacon," I said.

"I am going to the town of Mora. I can take you that far, then you have another seven miles to go," he said.

"Okay, thanks. Yes, I know. I used to live in Cleveland, down the road from Mora," I said.

As I settled in and buckled up, I turned and saw that the man was pointing a gun at me.

I was surprised how calm I felt when I saw the gun. I remained detached and calm. I thought: *This must be a fear of death test from my Meditation Master. If this body dies right now, I (the Soul) might as well Think and See Restoratively and concentrate my mind on the Beloved Divine Energy of the Universe within this man, seeing him as my own Mother, so I will go to the abode of Eternal Joy if this body is meant to perish. I might as well offer selfless service and be an instrument for this man to receive compassionate listening and empathy on the way, because he must be in pain if he is holding up a gun.*

I moved my mala prayer beads from my wrist and gently, quietly placed my right hand on my right knee. I pointed the beads toward the driver so they mirrored the aim of the gun.

I sat back, relaxed, and concentrated my mind on seeing the man as my own Mother. Focusing on the Beloved Divine Energy in him, I said something using the language of the heart, called compassionate communication.

"I see you are holding a gun toward me. Are you feeling concerned and needing safety and protection?"

"Yes," he said. "I want to be generous and give people rides around here, but I'm afraid of drug addicts who might want to stab me with heroin needles and steal money to buy drugs and alcohol."

He went on about all the violence he was facing in his village. He told me about the turbulence with his neighbors and his own family as we drove down the two-lane highway close to where I used to live in Hummingbird Community, studying the art of conscious co-creation.

I listened quietly and persisted in trying to see the man as my own Mother, clicking my mala prayer beads as loudly as I could while I had my mantra aimed at him. It helped me stay alert, compassionate, courageous, and in touch with the truth that Beloved Divine Energy in the Soul is eternal.

After several minutes, I responded with my guesses: "You must be torn because you want to be generous and serve travelers who pass through the community. Yet you are also nervous about safety and concerned about increasing substance abuse violence. You really want there to be peace, security, and harmony here. Is that it?"

"Yeah, that's totally it," he said.

He went into more detail about the violence in his village of Mora. I listened for another ten minutes, with the gun still pointed at me, loudly clicking my prayer beads one mantra at a time as I focused on the Beloved Divine Energy flowing through the man— rather than focusing on our differences.

When he finished talking about a violent family feud, I wondered out loud, "So, you sound upset about alcohol and drug violence going on between your relatives, and you want to see more safety, compassion, and justice here in this rural village area. Is that it?"

"Yes," said the man. Then he asked, "So what do you do, Srinath?"

"Well, I live with what possessions I can carry on my own back. I practice selfless service and meditation, mostly working on racial justice, building restorative systems, learning to host restorative circles, and serving Mother Earth. And I offer holistic empathy in villages, small communities, and schools. And I want to work in youth jails to share meditation."

I continued, "Now I'm going on a spiritual pilgrimage to a Lakota Sun Dance to support and serve my Aunty Pat who is dancing and my sister Lyla who is praying in the Women's Moon Circle Tent. I'm planning to lend a hand wherever it's needed in the kitchen."

The man's eyes expressed an interest in hearing more, so I went on, still hanging on tightly to my prayer mala.

"My spiritual Mother has embraced over thirty-five million people, and She considers each and every human being to be Her own child. She tirelessly offers humanitarian and community-building projects to feed the homeless on the streets through Mother's Kitchen, shares Integrated Amrita Meditation with youth in prisons, supports indigenous communities in villages in India, and supports disaster relief projects like donating a million dollars to embrace the devastation after Hurricane Katrina."

"Hearing all this, I don't think I need this gun out anymore," the man said.

And he put it away in the glove box.

"In fact, I'd like to drive fourteen miles out of my way, all the way to Chacon, to support you in your selfless service at this Lakota Sun Dance."

"Thanks," I said calmly.

In this way, the man and I ended up transforming gun violence, together.

—SRINATH WAIDLER-BARKER

*Simple inattention kills empathy,
let alone compassion. So the first step in
compassion is to notice the other's need. It all
begins with the simple act of attention.*

—DANIEL GOLEMAN

Feeling Out of Place

At a professional training focused on new education models, I was working in groups along with about twenty-five other people. We were doing a lot of experiential work, but some of the instructions were unclear. For example, a facilitator for one activity gave very muddled instructions for a task that had to do with expressing the nature of education somehow.

The man next to me raised his hand and said he didn't understand what was being asked of the group.

The facilitator repeated the instructions and kept trying to explain, but it still didn't make sense.

I didn't think the man who asked for help felt any clearer than I did. When I don't understand an activity, I usually go rogue and do whatever seems fun or relevant to me. But when I looked at the man, I could see his frustration and tension.

He was shaking his head and seemed stressed. When we were told to get started, I began to empathize with him, rather than try to make sense of what we were supposed to do.

"I can see that you're really stressed. Is that right?"

"Yeah!" he replied. "I'm totally overwhelmed and confused about what to do."

I reflected back his words.

"Okay. You're overwhelmed and confused—you don't know what's going on here."

He nodded.

"Is there more?" I asked.

He said he felt alienated in the room and was ready to leave. He felt excluded, like he didn't really belong. And he repeated that he was seconds from walking out.

"Wow!" I exclaimed. "You're ready to walk out!"

"Yeah. I feel really disconnected here," he said. "These people aren't my people. They're progressives. They're all white. I'm not. They have a certain mentality. I don't belong here."

I repeated back, "Okay, you're disconnected because it seems like the people here aren't your kind of people."

"I'm feeling all this anxiety. It's really making me sad. Actually, I feel downright resentful of these people. I'm pretty irritated!"

I kept reflecting back my understanding of what he was saying, and it seemed to work for him. He kept nodding his head and continued talking.

After several minutes, he took a breath and said in a calmer voice, "I do realize that part of this is my own story—that these people are so different from me. Maybe I'm just telling myself this, but I'm actually judging the folks around me."

"Well, what are you needing here, do you think?" I asked.

He began to talk again.

The table where we sat was supplied with markers, sticky notes, and big sheets of paper, so while he spoke I jotted down some of his main points: overwhelmed, alienated, anxious.

We were tasked to do something around how we felt about education, so I figured, *Hey, let's use this thing that's happening right now!* He watched me write, and when I asked about his needs, all we had to do was look at the notes.

He was confused and wanted to feel connected. He had

225

anxiety, and behind it was a need for ease. We kept going for twenty minutes or so—talking, translating, and writing. He was pouring out his heart and his pain. He needed inclusion, belonging, flexibility, and a sense of ownership.

All I did was reflect back what he said and write it down. Before long, we had a huge piece of paper filled with words.

"Well, we're supposed to make a kind of symbol of our ideas here. What do you think about a tree of empathy?" I asked.

"Oh! That's what that is! This is really helping!"

He seemed to feel more connected and relaxed.

We put together our empathy tree with all the pain words and needs written on different sticky notes—all of these made up the "leaves," some of which were composting at the base of the tree.

Our time was up, and as we wrapped up the activity, everyone around the room had an opportunity to share. I simply said we created an empathy tree, which grew out of our discussion. But he stood up, so animated and eloquent, and talked about how well the experience went.

"Whatever Edwin did was so great . . . I was ready to walk out of here! I was so pissed off, but he really listened!"

The energy in the room changed as he described our process. I could feel a sense of being grounded, a sense of connection as he shared what we did. It seemed everyone was amazed by the open way he spoke.

He kept referring to me and saying that what I did brought the change, so people were whispering in my direction, "What did you do? What was this magic that you did with him?"

I smiled and said, "I just empathized with him! Seriously, that's it!"

Experiencing the power of simple empathy was a high point for me. The facilitator kept trying to *explain* but couldn't hear where we were coming from. Listening makes all the difference sometimes. I really try to remember that.

—EDWIN RUTSCH, http://cultureofempathy.com

To practice NVC, we need to proceed slowly, think carefully before we speak, and often just take a deep breath and not speak at all. Learning the process and applying it both take time.

—MARSHALL B. ROSENBERG, PhD

Silent Empathy at the DMV

It looked to be a nonstop, hectic day, starting with a visit to the Department of Motor Vehicles to replace my driver's license. My license had been stolen, along with my wallet, a week earlier. I wasn't looking forward to standing in the DMV's infamously long lines, but I had my coffee and was ready to take care of business. As I approached the front door with my travel mug, the security guard stopped me.

"Ma'am," he said, "you cannot bring that in here, you know."

I sighed, audibly. I needed the mug of coffee to get me through the wait! I felt mad, but I had to comply.

"Okay," I replied, my frustration apparent. "Can I finish it in the doorway?"

He nodded, so I finished it and proceeded inside, thinking to myself, *Why is this security guard such a jerk? It's early, and people need their coffee!*

I took a number and sat down to wait my turn. As I waited, still irritated, I looked at the security guard and wondered what the job must be like for him. I noticed most of the people at the DMV seemed grumpy, and my thoughts shifted. *It must be challenging to deal with so many frustrated people all the time. He probably bears the brunt of their frustration all too often.*

As I put myself in his shoes, my initial irritation disappeared. A wave of gentle compassion and love for him washed over me. My frustration dissipated entirely.

Being around snappy people day in and day out must be discouraging and disheartening. Was he burned out from this job where no one looks forward to visiting? Did he need more acceptance, appreciation, consideration, and integrity—from people like me?

Soon I heard my number and I jumped up to approach the counter, ready to get on with my day. The clerk processed my paperwork and said she needed my twenty-five-dollar payment in cash.

Frantic, I said, "What? All I have is a credit card. I need to get this done today!"

She looked at me and shrugged.

I took a deep breath, put my hand over my heart, and reminded myself it would be okay. This would get taken care of, I told myself, either in the moment or sometime soon. In that split second, I flashed through struggles of the past and realized my issue was anything but earth-shattering. I breathed deeply again and reached for my wallet to see how much cash I had.

Two dollars short.

I looked at the clerk beseechingly. "I'm so close! I have almost enough money!"

She smiled, apologetically. "Ma'am, you'll have to submit the exact amount now or come back when you have it. . . . Next."

I stood there, frozen.

The security guard came over and asked, "Is there a problem, ma'am?"

I sheepishly told him I was trying to pay a license replacement fee but that I was missing money.

"How much?" he asked briskly.

"Two dollars."

He reached in his wallet and put two dollars on the counter for me. My eyes popped as I stood there, speechless. I wanted to hug him! I began my morning annoyed at this grumpy guy who wouldn't let me drink my coffee inside, but my experience transformed when I saw only his generosity and willingness to help.

I walked out of the DMV beaming, feeling supported and full of hope. Empathy had changed the day.

—NIKKI MARKMAN

> *When we focus on clarifying what is being*
> *observed, felt, and needed rather than on*
> *diagnosing and judging, we discover the depth of*
> *our own compassion.*

—MARSHALL B. ROSENBERG, PhD

Questioned by the Cops

I was on my way to a party with some of my college friends. We were planning to drink that night and I was carrying a container of alcohol from the car into the party house. I wasn't sure if the container was open or not—it was hard to tell.

There were cops at the house when we arrived and, before we got inside, an officer stopped me. He began asking me questions about the container. I wasn't sure if it was open or not, and I knew I might be in trouble, so I didn't know how to answer him.

The officer asked me for identification, but I kept hesitating. I could tell he thought I was lying to him. Usually I suppress my feelings because showing them feels like a sign of weakness, but when I pulled out my wallet, I told him I felt nervous and scared. I explained that I had hesitated to answer because of the vagueness of the rules.

I thought I would get in trouble, but he understood my uncertainty when I told him I was scared. He spent some time going over information about how to handle containers like the one I was holding. We ended up having a nice conversation.

—ANONYMOUS, www.nvcsantacruz.org

Empathy is the most radical of human emotions.

—GLORIA STEINEM

Jack's Funeral

When I arrived at Jack's funeral, I found the large church completely full. I recognized a lot of people and felt like I was among community. The only space left was standing room at the back. I sensed the solemnity among us as the coffin came in, followed by Jack's wife, Marie, and their two young sons.

I find all funeral services intensely moving because of the loss—the utter, irreversible loss—for those close to the person. And because of the power of death, the way it is beyond our grip, beyond our understanding. It makes visible the huge thing that is every person's life. All this, and the tragic experience of Jack's family, affected me in the first moments of the service.

I was very moved and felt a force rising up within me. I did my best to open myself and let the feelings flow. Sometimes this works for me—I can hold myself like the banks of a river while the feeling rushes through—but this time my river banks were dissolving, and the huge surge of feeling was fast becoming all that I was. Any moment now it would burst out as a wild, noisy outpouring. We were in England, where the culture for funerals involves weeping, certainly, but not loud shrieking and sobbing! *What to do?*

I looked toward the door and saw a route I could take that

231

would barely disturb anyone. I'd go outside. That would help. Just before leaving, I realized how much I wanted to be present, to be part of the service. Something within me resolved to find a way through this, and I remembered something I had recently learned. *With such a strong feeling, there must be an equally strong need underneath it. What could it be?*

From nowhere I could identify, an answer came immediately: I needed to worship. I was surprised. This was not something I had considered, and yet I was immediately calmed by this answer. This was it. It felt true. As I focused on my desire to worship, the forceful push of my feeling subsided, like a wave flowing into the ocean after breaking on the shore. I could feel my feet again. I could stand steady. I could stay in the church. I could worship. I fell into a deep state, totally centered and in sacredness for the rest of the service.

At the end there was an announcement that family and close friends would proceed to the burial in the cemetery a couple of miles away. I wondered whether I counted as a close friend. *Perhaps not,* I thought. I got on my bicycle and pedaled very slowly toward home—but something stopped me. I didn't feel ready to go home. Instead I headed to the house of a friend who had been at the funeral, but she was not home.

I paused, wondering what to do next. At least ten minutes had passed since the service ended, but I began cycling slowly toward the cemetery. I was in a deep state and could hear my inner promptings more clearly than usual, so I decided to trust my impulses for action in each moment. I cycled gently, at the exact speed that felt right to me, enjoying the spring flowers along the roadside in the dappled sunlight.

I arrived at the large cemetery, like a beautiful park in the May morning sunshine. In the distance I could see the funeral cars and the mourners beside the grave. I parked my bike and walked over to join them. Just as I arrived, the burial rituals were done, and people began embracing each other and talking quietly. I was glad

232

to embrace friends and participate in the moment, but sad to have missed the shared graveside prayers.

Marie and her sons were the first to depart from the group. They got into the leading funeral car and the group dispersed. No longer among the mourners, I wanted a moment to be with Jack, to connect with his spirit. I went close to the grave and looked down at the coffin, deep in the earth, where his body lay. I picked a few of the daisies growing abundantly in the grass and, with a prayer, threw them in. I stood in silence for several minutes.

Part of me felt continually alarmed. My mind was telling me I shouldn't do this—it wasn't right, not my place, not respectful. I was not nearly as close to him as the others. What would they think? But my inner connection was still very strong from my experience in the service, so I managed to stay with my inner promptings.

The last of the family and friends got into their cars and drove off slowly together. I stood alone next to Jack's grave. Then I felt like the moment was complete, but I was not ready to return to daily life. I saw a bench under a tree some distance away, so I walked over to it and sat down.

As the last car left the cemetery, I heard a motor start up. A small truck bounced over the grass to the grave. Two men got out and began spading earth onto Jack's coffin. They talked loudly as they worked, joking and chatting. They were full of the vigor of life. They reminded me of the gravediggers in Shakespeare's plays, contrasting life with death, humor with tragedy, lightness with sorrow. In a few efficient and energetic minutes, they had filled the grave and jumped on it to press the earth down, chatting cheerfully all the while. They threw their spades back into the trailer and drove off.

I sat for a while longer in the silence and stillness. It was done.

I did not see Marie during the next days. I had an urge to write to tell her what happened after she left, but I felt unsure. To send something so personal at such a sensitive time—would that be okay? Several days later I felt the urge again and, reconnecting to my decision to follow my inner impulses, I penned her a letter.

Some days later Marie rang me. With her voice full of joy, she told me how deeply grateful she was for my letter. She said she had left the graveside to care for her younger son when he could not take any more. Through the window of the car, she had watched me go to the grave, pick the flowers, throw them in, and stand in silent prayer. She told me she had been longing to do exactly this herself, and it was as if I had done it for her. It also meant a lot to her that I had seen the grave filled. It brought her solace and completion.

I was amazed. I had never considered that I might be doing it for her. From that moment in the church when I became deeply connected with myself, everything had flowed at the right time, right place, and right way. It was like grace, and I felt privileged to have been part of it.

—BRIDGET BELGRAVE, www.liferesources.org.uk

When you make the [human] connection,
the problem solves itself.

—MARSHALL ROSENBERG, PhD

Sidewalk Connection

I was walking along a main street in downtown Berkeley when I noticed a man in a doorway who had apparently slept outside the night before. I saw that he had a sleeping bag and other belongings gathered in his space. As I approached, he bolted up and began talking to himself loudly, swearing. He sounded pretty upset.

I felt a little scared as I watched him pace the sidewalk, waving his arms. My instinct was to cross the street to avoid him, so I slowed down to consider my options. I was about to walk around him when something caught my ear. I stopped. *Wait, what is he saying?* It was barely audible from that distance. Something about his shoes.

I took a few steps closer.

"Motherfucker! You had to take my fucking shoes! I'm a size fifteen! Those fucking shoes . . . Do you know how hard it was to get those motherfucking shoes! Asshole! Why don't you come here and show your face!"

I saw that he was, indeed, in his socks, walking in circles and gesturing to no one in particular. I felt terrible that he'd lost a pair of shoes, especially since it looked like he had so few things to begin with.

I wanted to do something, but I also wanted to feel safe. I had an idea. I saw a four-foot high brick wall nearby, marking the entrance to the underground train station. I walked to the other side of the wall to give myself a bit of a distance.

A concept I had just learned in a Nonviolent Communication training flashed through my mind. We practiced matching someone's energy as part of listening deeply to them. So that's what I tried to do.

"Hey there!" I yelled in the man's direction, mirroring his tone as best I could. "Are you so fucking pissed because someone took your shoes? Argh!"

He came closer. "Yeah! They're size fifteen!" He threw up his hands in frustration.

"Yeah! It's really hard to get that size!"

"Exactly, yes!" He sighed and paused for a moment, then revved up again.

"They're such cowards!" he said, and continued for several minutes about how spineless the person was who took his shoes.

"Do you wish they'd be straight up, that they'd show up and face you?" I asked.

"They're cowards!" he replied.

"And you want a chance to talk to them, to *do* something? Is that it?"

"Yeah!" He looked at me for a moment, taking a breath. "Grr!"

"God. Argh!" I threw up my hands. "Are you just so, *Argh*, as you think about it?"

"Yes!" he said, now fully facing me. "Yes, I am!"

We went on like this for a while, him repeating this need to

"EMPATHY NOTS"
Example

STORY COLLUSION

"What a jerk."
"You're totally right."

see the shoe thief face-to-face, and me reflecting his outrage. I guessed he felt hopeless and helpless, and that his need for the thief to show up and face him had something to do with power and resolution.

After a few minutes, his tone dropped abruptly.

"I don't know why I'm yelling. You seem like a really nice lady. I'm so sorry," he muttered.

I was stunned. "No! What? You don't need to be sorry. I would be upset too."

"Yeah, I really am," he replied, calmly.

"I can't buy you another pair of shoes but if you want a couple bucks for a sandwich or something, I'd be happy to buy you some lunch," I offered.

"No, thanks. I'm just too mad right now."

He went back into his anger, yelling at the sky and occasionally glancing in my direction, while I stood listening. With occasional nods, I stayed with his ups and downs.

"Yeah, you're still upset. These basics are important! This isn't resolved for you, yet, and that's frustrating!"

He seemed a bit more settled, and I was feeling done, so I began to say goodbye.

As I gathered up my things to leave, he made full eye contact.

"Hey, maybe I will take that couple bucks for a sandwich. That still okay?" he asked.

I gave him five dollars and as I went on my way, I could hear him talking to himself, but in a different voice than before.

I walked away feeling a sense of connection with this stranger. I appreciated the moments when he acknowledged my care for him. *You seem like such a nice lady.* I took that with me, glad that I found a way to connect with him safely and meaningfully.

—REHANA KADERALI

*Each of us carries some wisdom waiting to be
discovered at the center of our experience,
and everything we meet, if faced and held,
reveals a part of that wisdom.*

—MARK NEPO

Loser (Self-Empathy for a Slur)

It was like a blow,
I felt kicked in the stomach,
I felt shame,
And then I felt shame about feeling shame,
I know this isn't true, so why am I hurt?
It was late at night.

I had just been feeling good about the sci-fi novel I was working on. Then I saw the headline and read the *New York Times* article about the president's remarks. "President Trump described Haiti, El Salvador, and parts of Africa as 'shithole countries' in a meeting with lawmakers in the White House Thursday."

I know this isn't true, so why am I hurt?

I tried to talk myself out of it. *What he says should not matter to me. I have inside me the hills of Haiti, how it feels to walk the streets through Les Cayes, the colorful buildings, my family, growing up soaked in Haitian Kreyol, Haitian music, plantains, rice and beans.*

That self-talk didn't affect the imprint of the punch that held my mind, body, and heart knotted in pain.

I gathered myself to focus on being with the feelings inside.

How do I hold myself tenderly here? With some effort, I turned toward the pain with curiosity, looking for the need, trying to understand it. That moment was a departure from the useless pattern of judgment—alternating between judgment of self and judgment of the attacker.

Instead, I turned toward the pain, holding my vulnerability with caring interest.

It was hard to stay steady and feel it.

I could have gotten lost in thinking and intellectualizing, but instead I felt into the tension in my chest and the fear enveloping my torso.

It's a need for safety and respect.

At first the need for safety was strongest.

Then I noticed the shame was emanating from a part of me that believed him.

To believe that insult—the horror!

Part of me believed it.

Oh no, throw that part away. Reject it, bury it.

I acknowledged it. Then the commitment I had made to love all parts of myself unconditionally rose to the surface. I didn't want to pretend I was someone different, more evolved, healthier—I've developed faith that the truth leads to real healing. Looking for the beauty in what appears ugly, I hold myself with compassion there. *But how do I love myself?*

I asked the question: *What's the need met by believing in Trump's framework?*

I listened to the sensations and my emotions.

I sat still, listening patiently, receptively discovering a tidal wave inside urging me to agree with Trump's pronouncement.

Was it wanting ease? This force didn't want to fight. It insisted my whole body and soul contort into a ball. And with that awareness, a lot of mental energy, thoughts pummeling various versions of *no no no no no* at that urge to double into the fetal position and give up.

I felt into the energy of my aversion. What was the need of the venom that rose in response to the tidal wave urging me to give up?

Self-respect, dignity.

Dignity, I sighed. Dignity was so different from the soup I was swimming in. Light and loose, dignity circled like a bird above the sea.

Back to the tidal wave toward collapse. Could I hold myself without judgment, sit here with it?

Touching it again, memories flowed through my mind, so much heartbreak. I felt the exhaustion, the impression of a never-ending battle.

Oh God, is this too much?

I checked in, it was within my ability to listen.

My listening was more important than my believing.

Back to the body, holding the feelings,

Back to the energy,

The thoughts so loud, pulling me away from the body:

Answering and questioning, figuring out how to be right. *He's bad! Evil. Condemn him.* Thoughts of what's wrong with him and them—THEM!—all the thems.

And the shrill *What's wrong with me?*

The mind continues like a whirlwind. I will myself to dip below.

I repeated the word *compassion* out loud to myself for myself, beaming the word into the soup I found myself in. Like a beam of light from a lighthouse at night on a sea, the light of compassion stroked the tidal wave of pain.

Energy and emotion vibrating through the body, magnetically pulled by the need for ease and peace.

So then,

Continuing to feel,

The venom softened.

I felt tender and sweet with the pain that remained around my torso.

It was a great relief when the tears came.

I was engulfed but without the self-attack.

Swimming with the tidal wave formed by so many overwhelming losses,

No longer questioning her right to exist,

Her right to give up, surrender—a strategy for peace,

Her right to react however she wanted to react,

Somewhere that night, giving up turned into letting be, and she wasn't constricting me anymore into a ball.

Poison melted into more spaciousness.

And I stood by the living breathing experience of me.

Calmer. Peaceful. Clear.

And then my thoughts weren't coming from the intention to cut myself off from the pain,

Or to attack,

And this flowed:

Losers and winners,

The urge to condemn the current winner in the White House so strong,

To win somehow.

Now I'm more at peace, so I'm looking at the game,

"Don't hate the playa, hate the game,"

Is Haiti a loser or winner?

Modern life,

I play the game,

I pray and meditate, realizing moments of transcendence,

But I believe in the game,

The proof is in my fear,

I want to win and I don't want to lose!

What is winning?

Death is certain, but the urge for a better life drives me from sunrise to sunrise.

Where are ideals, values, and integrity?

The stuff of children's movies, 1950s sitcoms and comic books.

Will good triumph?

In superhero stories, winning at the end is proof that you are magic, right, and good.

Reality brims with decent hardworking people who lose a lot,

Good people who fail,

Innocent people who are oppressed and murdered, randomly, stupidly, relentlessly.

They lost. Who won?

The river of blood woven into American history . . . world history.

The wars, murders, oppression and enslavement.

It's the backdrop I usually ignore because otherwise I drown in meaninglessness.

There's so much to ignore, passing by the homeless mother and child staring desperately at me and the rich, well-dressed executive staring blankly at his iPhone.

In order for there to be winners, there have to be losers.

Will I be on the right side of the bell curve this time?

Next time?

—PHOENIX SOLEIL, www.phoenixsoleil.org

You never really understand a person until you consider things from his point of view.

—HARPER LEE

Reframing the Unthinkable

At the end of teaching a two-hour workshop, a participant, Allison, approached me and said a friend had prompted her to introduce herself. This was her second workshop with me on empathy and connection skills, and she wanted to share an experience she had after hearing a participant ask, "Can we really use this stuff after a couple hours?"

With an earnest face, she told me this "connection stuff" saved her life.

She told me she had been robbed while at home with her boyfriend. As one of the thieves held a gun to her head, she found herself thinking, *Wow, I wonder what kind of childhood this guy must have had to end up here.*

She looked him in the eye and felt only compassion. She didn't say anything, but she was surprised that her thoughts went to such a place in that moment. The robber made eye contact with her, then pulled his gun away. Her boyfriend was shot in the foot as the robbers fled, so she knew they were not afraid to use their weapons.

She wanted me to know how much she appreciated receiving the insight to care about another human being, no matter what.

Allison credited her remembrance of empathy as the tool that saved her life. She wanted me to know that a two-hour workshop could make all the difference in the world. It did to her.

—CAROL CHASE

This quality of understanding requires one of the most precious gifts one human being can give to another: our presence in the moment.

—MARSHALL B. ROSENBERG, PhD

Left Behind

I was sitting on my lanai (Hawaiian word for "porch") one morning having breakfast and enjoying solitude, when I suddenly heard what sounded like a conflict between a mom and her child.

"You come with me right now!" I heard a woman say.

I couldn't quite hear the girl's exact response, but the tone was definitely along the lines of "I don't want to."

As I listened, things got louder. Then all I could hear was the child's voice screaming over and over again, "Don't leave me, don't leave me, don't leave me!"

Two things happened inside of me. First, I thought about what it was like to be a small, scared child whose mom (apparently) just walked away. I thought about how much that girl might be needing security, connection, and reassurance.

Second, I realized I was scared too. I was worried the little girl might be in danger, but I was afraid to do anything about it because getting in between a parent and a child is tricky business. I didn't know the bigger story between this mom and her daughter, and I really like to be respectful of parents.

The screaming continued, though, and I couldn't help myself. I followed the sound, motivated by a sense of protection, to check things out. I rounded the corner in my rural neighborhood and saw the girl. She appeared to be no more than four years old and was totally freaking out. She was beside herself, and because I was a stranger to her, I approached carefully so I wouldn't scare her more.

I was about fifteen feet away when I sat on the ground. I looked at her and she saw me. But she kept staring ahead, yelling, "Don't leave me, don't leave me."

"Sounds like you're really scared," I said.

"No! I'm not scared!"

I nodded and replied, "Oh, you're really feeling mad."

She said, "Yeah, I'm mad!"

"You wish your mom was here."

She affirmed, "I want my mom to be here. I don't want her to leave me."

I thought this was pretty remarkable for a four-year-old to have such clarity of her needs. So I stayed right with what she was saying.

"Yeah, so you wish your mom was here and you wish she hadn't left you," I said.

She nodded, so I said, "It's a little scary for you to be left alone."

This time, my guess resonated. She softened and said, "Yeah, I'm scared."

Her voice lowered and she seemed to be shifting toward calm. Neither of us moved. Maintaining the distance between us, I continued to stay with her words. Soon we began to talk about how she wanted her mom, how she was hungry for breakfast, and about the doll in her clutch.

After a few minutes of chatting, I asked, "Would you like me to take you to your mom?"

She immediately went back into rage.

"NO!"

"Oh, okay," I said. "So you really want your mom to come to you."

"Yeah, yeah," she said.

I imagined she was scared that some stranger was going to try to take her somewhere, and I didn't blame her at all for that. So we waited and kept talking.

About that time, Mom showed up. I introduced myself and smiled reassuringly, figuring she was wondering why I was talking to her little girl.

"Sounds like you guys have been having a rough morning."

She sighed in acknowledgment. "Hard day. I haven't been able to get her to do anything I want."

"Yeah," I said. "It's really frustrating when we can't get the kind of cooperation that we need."

The mom smiled a little. We kept this empathic dialogue going for a few minutes while I shared about a parenting practice group I cofacilitate and she worked to carve a hole in a coconut for her daughter. The mom seemed more at ease, more alert, and after a bit, she motioned to her daughter to come along so they could go eat more breakfast.

As the mom started walking away, guess what happened? The little girl began to get angry all over again.

I said to the girl, "Oh, something's going on for you again."

"Yeah . . . ," she replied.

And then Mom stepped in and made an empathy guess of her own. She looked at her daughter and said, "Would you like to lead the way to the house, so we can eat?"

Her little girl took a breath and said, "Yes, yes."

She took her mom's hand and led her down the driveway without a backward glance toward me. This is the level of cooperation I love to see between parents and kids.

—JIM MANSKE, www.radicalcompassion.com

Imagine you are walking in the woods and you see a small dog sitting by a tree. As you approach it, it suddenly lunges at you, teeth bared. You are frightened and angry. But then you notice that one of its legs is caught in a trap. Immediately your mood shifts from anger to concern: You see that the dog's aggression is coming from a place of vulnerability and pain. This applies to all of us. When we behave in hurtful ways, it is because we are caught in some kind of painful trap. The more we look through the eyes of wisdom at ourselves and each other, the more we cultivate a compassionate heart. It is such a blessing to forgive!

—TARA BRACH

Zeke and the KKK

Sixteen-year-old Zeke was an active member of the Ku Klux Klan. I met him when I was teaching a two-day workshop on nonviolence for high schoolers in the San Francisco Bay Area. The first day of the workshop, we focused on how to transcend fixed ideas and perceptions of others while considering their human needs. On the second day, we worked on conflict resolution skills, but we also really wanted to support the connections between students.

Zeke was uncomfortable with all of this, and by the second day, he had sat with his discomfort long enough. In a room full of people he saw as Jewish, gay, black, liberal, the wrong kind of white, and female, he had trouble keeping quiet. When it was revealed that a Jewish girl's sister was getting married to another woman, he couldn't help saying what was on his mind.

"That's just wrong!" he exclaimed.

"Are you uncomfortable because there are people in here you're not used to connecting with?" I asked.

In response, Zeke explained why he thought certain people were simply "born inferior." His monologue agitated several people in the room, but he continued.

"I hate these people, but you know, don't get me wrong. I'm not a violent person. I wouldn't want harm to come to them. It's just that I hate certain people."

"Hmm," I replied. "Now I'm confused, because you're saying you hate these people, yet you don't want any harm to come to them. I'm guessing you might even have some confusion about your feelings toward these people. Because you say you don't want to be violent, yet you speak of hate."

Zeke listened with his arms folded across his chest, his eyes fixed on mine.

I continued, "I'm also confused about your choice to be a member of the KKK. From what I know, they have created a lot of violence against the folks you say you hate. Can you tell me why you're a member? What was your primary motivation to join?"

Zeke looked straight into me and said, "My dad is a member of the KKK!"

The others bristled with comments.

One student chimed in, "Ah man, just 'cause your dad's a hater doesn't mean you gotta be one too!"

Nodding at that profound statement, I looked into Zeke's eyes as intensely as he had looked into mine and reflected what I heard.

"I'm hearing how much you'd like to connect to your dad. I am also hearing that maybe you feel conflicted about being a member of an organization that tries to create connection through violence and hating others."

Leaning toward Zeke, trying to tangibly soften the room with my presence, I asked, "Has this really met your need to connect with your father?"

"Yeah, I guess I joined 'cause I hoped to get closer to my dad. I just wanted to get along with him," he replied, looking a little unsteady.

Zeke's eyes swelled but he did not want to cry, not in front of this group. He paused, breathed in fully, and then exhaled audibly, trying to regain his composure. I wasn't sure if he was affected by the gravity of this new awareness or if he merely wanted to hold back his tears.

It didn't matter. The wheels were already in motion.

When Zeke sat for a little longer in this empathic connection, which afforded him the opportunity to link up his mind with his heart, he realized that he had not joined the KKK because he hated certain people. Rather, he was desperate to find a way to connect with his father.

We carried on with the day, but he walked up to me after the workshop and said, "You know, that was the first time I felt fear begin to leave my body. I'm actually relieved."

With his new clarity, he began to assess the effectiveness of his choice, and he decided that hating others was truly not his path, not an expression of his authentic presence. He was able to get past the enemy images his mind had created about some of these other people—and the fixed ideas he had about himself—to see what he really needed. Zeke ultimately decided to quit the KKK. He developed new friendships. And he continued to work on various other strategies to find connection with his dad.

—CATHERINE CADDEN, www.zenvc.org

Appendix A

Habitual Versus Empathic Responses—Reference Sheet

C onversational habitual responses are normal and may be
the default setting when a new Nonviolent Communication
practitioner is listening to someone who is upset. It might be
useful to think of default responses as "empathy nots" because
of how disconnecting they can be when used unconsciously or
generically.

Nonviolent Communication practitioners learn the impact
of listening more empathically—with warm presence and non-
attachment to the course of the conversation—and guiding the
dialogue with this implicit question in mind: *What's important to
this person?*

This reference sheet is designed for those interested in
developing the empathy muscle. The conversational choices
outlined below illustrate nuances between different responses.
Rather than relying on habitual responses, choosing an empathic
response may be more appropriate and connecting.

	Habitual Response ("Empathy Not")	Empathy Tip	Empathic Response
Educating	He's just doing his best. It's hard for people who grew up in his situation to not get defensive hearing feedback.	Keep your focus on what they're saying until they request your opinion.	So it's painful and unproductive to talk with him when he's that upset. That's hard.
Advice	You know, I read that 70 to 85 percent of fertility issues can be shifted with nutritional changes. You should give that a try.	Recognize your desire to help or fix, but stay with them in their unfolding story.	Wow, so you're really wondering if there's anything you can do for your body.
Reassurance	I think you did a good job at the pitch. Don't worry, you're doing fine on the new team.	Guess a feeling that might be up for them.	Is it that you're worried about your job or just that you felt vulnerable today?
Coaching	I want to invite you to take a breath right now . . .	Wait until they ask for suggestions.	Sounds like things seem really over-whelming right now!
Sympathy	I hate it when that happens! I'm so pissed! You don't deserve that.	Note to yourself how their story triggers you, but keep the spotlight on them.	You're furious about the email she sent! You all worked hard and decided on a plan already!
Spiritualizing	These things always happen for a reason.	Guess what they might be needing and see if it resonates.	You're needing some sign that it will work itself out? Something about hope?
Colluding (Agreeing or Disagreeing)	You're right about him being irresponsible. He's so immature.	Reflect back (recap) what you're hearing without agreeing it's the truth.	So part of you is concerned he won't come through. Ugh.
Evaluating	I think it's good that you told your kids what's going on. It's healthy for them to know!	Trust they'll find their own truth, organically, without you directing the process.	Sounds like you're second-guessing how you presented this to the kids? But you definitely wanted to be honest as possible with them?
Storytelling	I know what you mean! That's exactly what my wife does. She always manages to . . .	Keep it about them until they're done. Then share if they have space to listen.	So she was upset and you ended up feeling guilty? Even though you'd warned her about the traffic?

Appendix B

Empathy Skill Practice

U sually, we think of offering empathy as something we do off-the-cuff when someone's upset. We weave a little empathy into some dialogue with an angry stranger, a friend, or a sad lover. Practicing empathy skills with someone in a *planned* way, however, is a great idea for more formal, deliberate learning. It is one of the best strategies I know to change those default habitual responses ("empathy nots") and to practice more mindful, empathic connections.

Practicing empathy the way it's described in this book is countercultural and feels a little unnatural for most people. Changing the way you think and talk can take some effort and mindfulness. In a longer-term Nonviolent Communication program, you might be assigned an "empathy buddy" to practice with. But this is something you can also create for yourself with a willing partner.

Here's how it works: Set aside time to talk with your empathy buddy (in person, by phone, or by video call) weekly for twenty to sixty minutes total. You'll spend half the time being listened to as you share whatever's going on for you in that moment—good or bad, happy or sad. You can share anything. While your partner tries to listen empathically, notice how it feels to be heard in this way—how well it works or doesn't work for you.

When it's your turn to be the listener, try to practice *not* giving your buddy advice and *not* reassuring them. Instead, begin by focusing on three basic skills:

1. **Reflecting back**, or recapping, the gist of what they're saying.
2. **Guessing the feelings** that are going on for them.
3. **Guessing the needs** connected to those feelings.

These can be challenging skills to master, especially when the other person is upset or all over the place. The process is not exactly linear and can definitely feel mechanical during the earlier attempts. But it is a good, concrete place to start.

To help the process along, I've created a checklist to support you during *planned exchanges* when you want to practice offering empathy. Every conversation will call for different skills, so the purpose of the checklist is *not* to check off all the boxes, but to use it as a guide to explore what works. The goal is to help the empathy receiver feel more understood and self-connected, which might be accomplished with as little as five minutes of warm, quiet listening from the giver. It all depends! This tool is intended to support mindfulness, not create a rigid prescription.

The Empathy Giver (the listener):
- I showed up with warm presence.
- I offered a recap.
- I offered a guess of their feelings or needs.
- I asked about body sensations.
- I offered one digestible guess at a time.
- I tried to let the receiver's rhythm determine the pace of my guesses.
- I felt comfortable hearing that a guess didn't resonate.
- I noticed when I felt compelled to mention a strategy or give advice.

- I let my partner know if I was "full" or triggered.
- I wrapped up the session at the time we agreed upon.

The Empathy Receiver (the speaker):
- I made a request for a recap.
- I made a request for my feelings or needs to be guessed.
- I felt comfortable saying that a guess didn't resonate.
- I paused every so often to allow the giver a chance to speak and make their guesses.
- I connected more deeply with my feelings during the session.
- I connected more deeply with my needs during the session.
- I connected more to my body sensations during the session.
- A new idea, possibility, or strategy popped up organically during the session.
- I felt comfortable wrapping up a topic thread when I was complete.

Debrief:
- What worked well for me during this session was _____.
- What I noticed about myself in each role was _____.
- Next time, I'm hopeful that _____.

During your listening session, try to let go of thinking about the checklist or it could pull you out of the moment. You might experiment with having the checklist in front of you to reference either *before* or *after* a planned empathy exchange. If it feels helpful, use the checklist to track which skills were accessible for you during a given practice session as the empathy giver or receiver. You may:
- Intend to focus on a specific skill. (Example: *I'll try to make shorter empathy guesses and talk in shorter segments when I'm the receiver.*)
- Intend to notice progress over time. (Example: *Wow, making*

a needs guess is practically second nature these days! I don't even have to think about it like I used to!)

- Watch for trends. (Example: *Hmm, I often check off the same items, but so far I have not tuned into body sensations. Interesting—is that because I don't notice my body sensations at all during empathy or I just haven't brought it up verbally?)*

What if you don't know anyone who wants to be an empathy buddy, but you'd really like to practice? Here are a few suggestions:

- Tap into the network of a local Nonviolent Communication practice community for recommendations.
- Search for and join Nonviolent Communication–related groups online (such as Yahoo!, Google, or Facebook groups). Start a thread asking for suggestions. In some groups, it's normal to get empathy in writing straight from your post!
- Practice silently translating the complaints and judgments from your loved ones into feelings and needs. Just make the guess in your head without verbalizing anything.
- Practice translating your own complaints and judgments into feelings and needs.
- Consider getting someone's okay before offering formal empathy guesses. If you let them know ahead of time that you're trying something you recently learned, they likely won't be put off by your language. *Are you feeling X because you're needing Y?* isn't exactly a normal thing for most of us to hear.

Appendix C

Common Challenges and Helpful Tips

If you're excited to go out there and empathize your heart out, I've done my job. However, there are a few stumbling blocks that often come up for newbies. I'd like to offer some tips to make your learning curve gentler. The table below outlines different scenarios that might come up when practicing empathy, helpful tips to consider, and examples of empathic ways to respond.

Scenario	Empathy Tip	Empathic Response
You're attached to your empathy guesses being right and it's hard to hear that a guess is off. You: *Was some part of you scared in that moment?* Them: *No, not really.* You: *Oh . . . are you sure you weren't a little worried?*	It's normal to want to be right. And it feels good to be helpful! But it can also be valuable to hear what is *not* contributing to their distress. Narrowing down the guesses can be a gift, especially when someone is navigating something that feels vague or amorphous to them.	You: *Was some part of you scared in that moment?* Them: *No, not really.* You: *Okay, so fear isn't quite it.* Them: *It's actually a relief to know fear isn't part of this; anxiety used to be such a big issue for me.* You: *So you feel a tiny celebration that fear isn't in the mix?* Them: *Yeah, totally. I think it's more about boundaries and determination now.*

Scenario	Empathy Tip	Empathic Response
You're hesitant to make a guess unless you're pretty sure it's right. Or your mind goes blank from performance anxiety. Them: *So, anyway, I don't know what to think! Do you have any guesses for me?* You: *Umm. You already said you're mad. So, anger. Umm . . . I don't know.*	Self-consciousness is so normal, especially when you're learning something new that you really care about. But it's hard to be present when you're self-conscious. Bring your attention back to their words, take a breath, and let it be enough to bring warm attunement to what they're saying.	Them: *So anyway, I don't know what to think. Do you have any guesses for me?* You: *Hmm. [Deep breath.] You mentioned anger. Can I recap the main things I heard first? Just to make sure I got the gist of everything. That might help me get clearer.* Them: *Sure!*
They begin to explain why your empathy guess didn't resonate with them, but as they do, it sounds like they just didn't understand. You: *Were you needing integration?* Them: *No. I just wanted these parts to come together better. I wanted more union.* You: *That's what I meant about integration.*	It happens! Resist the urge to educate or explain why you guessed what you did. Let them pick the word that works for them and go with it. The key is that you understand what they're trying to convey, and that they're feeling heard!	You: *Were you needing integration?* Them: *No. I just wanted these parts to come together better. I wanted more union.* You: *Okay, so "union" is what clicks, huh? Got it.*
You think you should've done more or said more. You think you didn't help enough. You: *Was this about consideration?* Them: *I guess so. And now that I think about it, consideration actually comes down to reassurance. I'm just wanting some peace in this relationship! I want to trust it without question!*	Some people just need a tiny nudge to begin talking themselves all the way through their own process—guessing their feelings and needs, and coming up with spontaneous thoughts that resonate. Remember, if they feel understood and more in touch with themselves at the end of a conversation, it's a win!	You: *Was this about consideration?* Them: *I guess so. And now that I think about it, consideration comes down to reassurance. I'm just wanting some peace in this relationship! I want to trust it without question!!* You: *Wow, is it good to be in touch with all that?*

Appendixes

Scenario	Empathy Tip	Empathic Response
You feel mechanical in the way you're making guesses. Them: *I've just been feeling so devastated by this loss. I can't even begin to say.* You: *Are you feeling sad because you're needing connection?*	It's normal to feel awkward when trying to connect in this new way of listening. Be gentle with yourself as you practice new skills while expressing your care.	Them: *I've just been feeling so devastated by this loss. I can't even begin to say.* You: *Ugh, [nodding], just so sad.* Them: *Yeah. [Tearing up.]* You: *[Audible breath.] Yeah. Really missing that connection.* Them: *Yes! I don't have anyone right now!*
The other person doesn't seem to be enjoying the empathy you're offering. Somehow it doesn't seem to be clicking.	It might not be working for them, for whatever reason. Be willing to let it go if it's not clicking. See if you can sense what would be more connecting.	You: *Is this feeling helpful, me just listening like this? Or are you wanting something different?* Them: *Well, I guess I'd like to know if you've ever been in my shoes. Has this ever happened to you?* You: *Totally! I can tell you my story if you'd like.*
They don't like the way you're talking and it makes them uncomfortable. Them: *Why are you talking like that, anyway?* You: *You're confused and wanting clarity?* Them: *Stop it!*	Focusing on feelings and needs will make some people uncomfortable. They may worry they're being judged, taken advantage of, or handled in some way. Be transparent—let them know you're trying to connect. If they ask about your language, they may feel less connected rather than more. Adjust accordingly and see how it goes.	Them: *Why are you talking like that?* You: *Oh! Right. I guess I'm trying something from a book I read, but I'm a beginner. Is it a little off-putting?* Them: *Yeah, a little!* You: *Sorry. I really do care about what you were saying. Should we go back to where you left off?*

Scenario	Empathy Tip	Empathic Response
As a receiver, you feel annoyed by all the times you're NOT met with empathy. You: *It's all been a lot to sort through.* Them: *Why don't you try and set it up with a calendar app?* You: *Oh, yeah, I have one already. I just can't seem to get myself to follow through.* Them: *What about trying . . .* You: *This isn't empathy!*	It can be annoying to hear "empathy nots" when it's your turn to be heard. A quick request for listening might help. If not, you could try: • Seeking resources on self-empathy. • Finding an empathy buddy who wants to learn how to listen empathically. • Connecting with an online Nonviolent Communication group and getting some empathy there. • Offering a Nonviolent Communication book to your listener, if you sense they'd welcome that suggestion.	You: *It's all been a lot to sort through.* Them: *Why don't you try and set it up with a calendar app?* You: *Oh, yeah, I have one already. I just can't seem to get myself to follow through.* Them: *What about trying . . .* You: *Let me just stop you for a sec. Right now, I'm not ready for ideas. Do you have space just to listen a bit?* Them: *Sure, it's just that . . .* You: [Mentally switching into self-empathy: *I'm so wanting space to be heard. And I'm overwhelmed and frustrated that this feels so hard right now.*]

Clearly expressing
how **I am**
without blaming
or criticizing

Empathically receiving
how **you are**
without hearing
blame or criticism

OBSERVATIONS

1. What I observe *(see, hear, remember, imagine, free from my evaluations)* that does or does not contribute to my well-being:

   "When I (see, hear) . . . "

1. What you observe *(see, hear, remember, imagine, free from your evaluations)* that does or does not contribute to your well-being:

   "When you see/hear . . . "

   (Sometimes unspoken when offering empathy)

FEELINGS

2. How I feel *(emotion or sensation rather than thought)* in relation to what I observe:

   "I feel . . . "

2. How you feel *(emotion or sensation rather than thought)* in relation to what you observe:

   "You feel . . ."

NEEDS

3. What I need or value *(rather than a preference, or a specific action)* that causes my feelings:

   ". . . because I need/value . . . "

3. What you need or value *(rather than a preference, or a specific action)* that causes your feelings:

   ". . . because you need/value . . ."

Clearly requesting that
which would enrich **my**
life without demanding

Empathically receiving that
which would enrich **your** life
without hearing any demand

REQUESTS

4. The concrete actions I would like taken:

   "Would you be willing to . . . ?"

4. The concrete actions you would like taken:

   "Would you like . . . ?"

   (Sometimes unspoken when offering empathy)

Some Basic Feelings We All Have

Feelings when needs are fulfilled

- Amazed
- Comfortable
- Confident
- Eager
- Energetic
- Fulfilled
- Glad
- Hopeful
- Inspired
- Intrigued
- Joyous
- Moved
- Optimistic
- Proud
- Relieved
- Stimulated
- Surprised
- Thankful
- Touched
- Trustful

Feelings when needs are not fulfilled

- Angry
- Annoyed
- Concerned
- Confused
- Disappointed
- Discouraged
- Distressed
- Embarrassed
- Frustrated
- Helpless
- Hopeless
- Impatient
- Irritated
- Lonely
- Nervous
- Overwhelmed
- Puzzled
- Reluctant
- Sad
- Uncomfortable

 ## Some Basic Needs We All Have

Autonomy
- Choosing dreams/goals/values
- Choosing plans for fulfilling one's dreams, goals, values

Celebration
- Celebrating the creation of life and dreams fulfilled
- Celebrating losses: loved ones, dreams, etc. (mourning)

Integrity
- Authenticity • Creativity
- Meaning • Self-worth

Interdependence
- Acceptance • Appreciation
- Closeness • Community
- Consideration
- Contribution to the enrichment of life
- Emotional Safety • Empathy

Physical Nurturance
- Air • Food
- Movement, exercise
- Protection from life-threatening forms of life: viruses, bacteria, insects, predatory animals
- Rest • Sexual Expression
- Shelter • Touch • Water

Play
- Fun • Laughter

Spiritual Communion
- Beauty • Harmony
- Inspiration • Order • Peace

- Honesty (the empowering honesty that enables us to learn from our limitations)
- Love • Reassurance
- Respect • Support
- Trust • Understanding

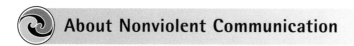

About Nonviolent Communication

Nonviolent Communication has flourished for more than four decades across sixty countries selling more than 1,500,000 books in over thirty languages for one simple reason: it works.

From the bedroom to the boardroom, from the classroom to the war zone, Nonviolent Communication (NVC) is changing lives every day. NVC provides an easy-to-grasp, effective method to get to the root of violence and pain peacefully. By examining the unmet needs behind what we do and say, NVC helps reduce hostility, heal pain, and strengthen professional and personal relationships. NVC is now being taught in corporations, classrooms, prisons, and mediation centers worldwide. And it is affecting cultural shifts as institutions, corporations, and governments integrate NVC consciousness into their organizational structures and their approach to leadership.

Most of us are hungry for skills that can improve the quality of our relationships, to deepen our sense of personal empowerment or simply help us communicate more effectively. Unfortunately, most of us have been educated from birth to compete, judge, demand, and diagnose; to think and communicate in terms of what is "right" and "wrong" with people. At best, the habitual ways we think and speak hinder communication and create misunderstanding or frustration. And still worse, they can cause anger and pain, and may lead to violence. Without wanting to, even people with the best of intentions generate needless conflict.

NVC helps us reach beneath the surface and discover what is alive and vital within us, and how all of our actions are based on human needs that we are seeking to meet. We learn to develop a vocabulary of feelings and needs that helps us more clearly express what is going on in us at any given moment. When we understand and acknowledge our needs, we develop a shared foundation for much more satisfying relationships. Join the thousands of people worldwide who have improved their relationships and their lives with this simple yet revolutionary process.

About PuddleDancer Press

PuddleDancer Press (PDP) is the main publisher of Nonviolent Communication™ related works. Its mission is to provide high-quality materials to help people create a world in which all needs are met compassionately. By working in partnership with the Center for Nonviolent Communication and NVC trainers, teams, and local supporters, PDP has created a comprehensive promotion effort that has helped bring NVC to thousands of new people each year.

Since 1998 PDP has donated more than 60,000 NVC books to organizations, decision-makers, and individuals in need around the world.

Visit the PDP website at www.NonviolentCommunication.com to find the following resources:

- **Shop NVC**—Continue your learning. Purchase our NVC titles online safely, affordably, and conveniently. Find everyday discounts on individual titles, multiple-copies, and book packages. Learn more about our authors and read endorsements of NVC from world-renowned communication experts and peacemakers. www.NonviolentCommunication.com/store/

- **NVC Quick Connect e-Newsletter**—Sign up today to receive our monthly e-Newsletter, filled with expert articles, upcoming training opportunities with our authors, and exclusive specials on NVC learning materials. Archived e-Newsletters are also available

- **About NVC**—Learn more about these life-changing communication and conflict resolution skills including an overview of the NVC process, key facts about NVC, and more.

- **About Marshall Rosenberg**—Access press materials, biography, and more about this world-renowned peacemaker, educator, bestselling author, and founder of the Center for Nonviolent Communication.

- **Free Resources for Learning NVC**—Find free weekly tips series, NVC article archive, and other great resources to make learning these vital communication skills just a little easier.

For more information, please contact PuddleDancer Press at:

2240 Encinitas Blvd., Ste. D-911 • Encinitas, CA 92024
Phone: 760-652-5754 • Fax: 760-274-6400
Email: email@puddledancer.com • www.NonviolentCommunication.com

The Center for Nonviolent Communication (CNVC) is an international nonprofit peacemaking organization whose vision is a world where everyone's needs are met peacefully. CNVC is devoted to supporting the spread of Nonviolent Communication (NVC) around the world.

Founded in 1984 by Dr. Marshall B. Rosenberg, CNVC has been contributing to a vast social transformation in thinking, speaking and acting—showing people how to connect in ways that inspire compassionate results. NVC is now being taught around the globe in communities, schools, prisons, mediation centers, churches, businesses, professional conferences, and more. Hundreds of certified trainers and hundreds more supporters teach NVC to tens of thousands of people each year in more than 60 countries.

CNVC believes that NVC training is a crucial step to continue building a compassionate, peaceful society. Your tax-deductible donation will help CNVC continue to provide training in some of the most impoverished, violent corners of the world. It will also support the development and continuation of organized projects aimed at bringing NVC training to high-need geographic regions and populations.

To make a tax-deductible donation or to learn more about the valuable resources described below, visit the CNVC website at www. CNVC.org:

- **Training and Certification**—Find local, national, and international training opportunities, access trainer certification information, connect to local NVC communities, trainers, and more.

- **CNVC Bookstore**—Find mail or phone order information for a complete selection of NVC books, booklets, audio, and video materials at the CNVC website.

- **CNVC Projects**—Participate in one of the several regional and theme-based projects that provide focus and leadership for teaching NVC in a particular application or geographic region.

- **E-Groups and List Servs**—Join one of several moderated, topic-based NVC e-groups and list servs developed to support individual learning and the continued growth of NVC worldwide.

For more information, please contact CNVC at:

9301 Indian School Rd., NE, Suite 204, Albuquerque, NM 87112-2861
Ph: 505-244-4041 • US Only: 800-255-7696 • Fax: 505-247-0414
Email: cnvc@CNVC.org • Website: www.CNVC.org

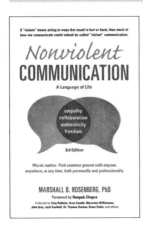

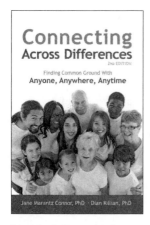

Connecting Across Differences, 2nd Edition

Finding Common Ground With Anyone, Anywhere, Anytime

By Jane Marantz Connor, PhD and Dian Killian, PhD

$19.95 – Trade Paper 6x9, 416pp
ISBN: 978-1-892005-24-3

Profound Connection Is Just a Conversation Away!

In this fully revised second edition, Dr. Dian Killian and Dr. Jane Marantz Connor offer a comprehensive and accessible guide for exploring the concepts, applications, and transformative power of the Nonviolent Communication process. Discover simple, yet transformative skills to create a life of abundance, where building the personal, professional, and community connections you long for begins with a simple shift in thinking.

Now with an expanded selection of broadly applicable exercises, role-plays, and activities that challenge readers to immediately apply the concepts in everyday life, this new edition opens the authors' insight to an even broader audience. Detailed and comprehensive, this combined book and workbook enhances communication skills by introducing the basic NVC model, as well as more advanced NVC practices.

Relevant, meaningful exercises follow each concept, giving readers the chance to immediately apply the skills they've learned to real life experiences.

Drawing on a combined 25 years of experience, the authors help readers to:

- Transform negative self-talk into self empowerment
- Foster trust and collaboration when stakes are high
- Establish healthy relationships to satisfy your needs
- Defuse anger, enemy images, and other barriers to connection
- Get what you want while maintaining respect and integrity

In each chapter, numerous exercises invite readers to apply NVC skills and concepts in their own lives. The second part features extensive dialogues illustrating NVC in action including in self-empathy, empathy, and mediation. The book closes with a resource guide for further learning and an interview with Marshall Rosenberg from the February 2003 *Sun Magazine*.

Available from PuddleDancer Press, the Center for Nonviolent Communication, all major bookstores, and Amazon.com. Distributed by Independent Publisher's Group: 800-888-4741.

SAVE an extra 10% at NonviolentCommunication.com with code: **bookads**

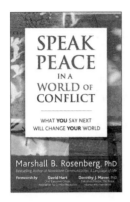

Speak Peace in a World of Conflict

What You Say Next Will Change Your World

By Marshall B. Rosenberg, PhD

$15.95 — Trade Paper 5-3/8x8-3/8, 208pp
ISBN: 978-1-892005-17-5

Create Peace in the Language You Use!

International peacemaker, mediator, and healer, Marshall Rosenberg shows you how the language you use is the key to enriching life. *Speak Peace* is filled with inspiring stories, lessons, and ideas drawn from more than forty years of mediating conflicts and healing relationships in some of the most war-torn, impoverished, and violent corners of the world. Find insight, practical skills, and powerful tools that will profoundly change your relationships and the course of your life for the better.

Discover how you can create an internal consciousness of peace as the first step toward effective personal, professional, and social change. Find complete chapters on the mechanics of Speaking Peace, conflict resolution, transforming business culture, transforming enemy images, addressing terrorism, transforming authoritarian structures, expressing and receiving gratitude, and social change.

Nonviolent Communication has flourished for more than four decades across sixty countries selling more than 1,500,000 books for a simple reason: it works.

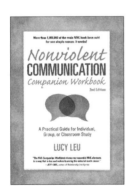

Nonviolent Communication
Companion Workbook, 2nd Edition

A Practical Guide for Individual, Group, or Classroom Study

By Lucy Leu

$21.95 — Trade Paper 7x10, 240pp
ISBN: 978-1-892005-29-8

Putting NVC Skills Into Practice!

Learning Nonviolent Communication has often been equated with learning a whole new language. The *NVC Companion Workbook* helps you put these powerful, effective skills into practice with chapter-by-chapter study of Marshall Rosenberg's cornerstone text, *NVC: A Language of Life*. Create a safe, supportive group learning or practice environment that nurtures the needs of each participant. Find a wealth of activities, exercises, and facilitator suggestions to refine and practice this powerful communication process.

Nonviolent Communication has flourished for more than four decades across sixty countries selling more than 1,500,000 books for a simple reason: it works.

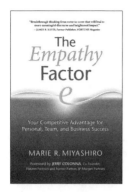

The Empathy Factor

Your Competitive Advantage for Personal, Team, and Business Success

By Marie R. Miyashiro, APR

$19.95 — Trade Paper 6x9, 256pp
ISBN: 978-1-892005-25-0

The Transformative Power of Empathy!

In this groundbreaking book, award-winning communication and organizational strategist Marie Miyashiro explores the missing element leaders must employ to build profits and productivity in the new economy—Empathy.

The Empathy Factor takes Dr. Marshall Rosenberg's work developing Compassionate Communication into the business community by introducing *Integrated Clarity*®—a powerful framework you can use to understand and effectively meet the critical needs of your organization without compromising those of your employees or customers.

"Breakthrough thinking from cover to cover. *The Empathy Factor* will help thoughtful business people add substance and dimension to relationships within the workforce—colleagues and customers."

—JAMES B. HAYES, Former Publisher, FORTUNE Magazine

Being Genuine

Stop Being Nice, Start Being Real

By Thomas d'Ansembourg

$17.95 — Trade Paper 5-3/8x8-3/8, 280pp
ISBN: 978-1-892005-21-2

A Fresh, New Perspective on Communication!

Being Genuine brings Thomas d'Ansembourg's blockbuster French title to the English market. His work offers you a fresh new perspective on the proven skills offered in the bestselling book, *Nonviolent Communication: A Language of Life.* Drawing on his own real-life examples and stories, Thomas d'Ansembourg provides practical skills and concrete steps that allow us to safely remove the masks we wear, which prevent the intimacy and satisfaction we desire with our intimate partners, children, parents, friends, family, and colleagues.

"Through this book, we can feel Nonviolent Communication not as a formula but as a rich, meaningful way of life, both intellectually and emotionally."

—Vicki Robin, cofounder, Conversation Cafes, coauthor, *Your Money or Your Life*

Words That Work In Business, Expanded

2nd Edition, *A Practical Guide to Effective Communication in the Workplace*

By Ike Lasater
With Julie Stiles

$12.95 – Trade Paper 5-3/8x8-3/8, 144pp
ISBN: 978-1-892005-01-4

Do You Want to Be Happier, More Effective, and Experience Less Stress at Work?

Do you wish for more respectful work relationships? To move beyond gossip and power struggles, to improved trust and productivity? If you've ever wondered if just one person can positively affect work relationships and company culture, regardless of your position, this book offers a resounding "yes." The key is shifting how we think and talk.

Former attorney-turned-mediator, Ike Lasater, offers practical communication skills matched with recognizable work scenarios to help anyone address the most common workplace relationship challenges. Learn proven communication skills to: Enjoy your workday more; effectively handle difficult conversations; reduce workplace conflict and stress; improve individual and team productivity; be more effective at meetings; and give and receive meaningful feedback.

Collaborating in the Workplace

A Guide for Building Better Teams

By Ike Lasater
With Julie Stiles

$7.95 – Trade Paper 5-3/8x8-3/8, 88pp
ISBN: 978-1-934336-16-8

Develop Crucial Skills to Help You and Your Teammates Connect With One Another in Ways That Foster Superior Collaboration!

What can individuals do to improve the ability of teams to collaborate and create powerful outcomes? Collaborating in the Workplace focuses on the key skills that research shows support effective collaboration and the practical, step-by-step exercises that individuals can practice to improve those skills. By using this book, people can work better together to create outstanding outcomes.

"A wonderfully practical guide for building teams and getting the best out of everyone. If you are looking to build collaboration in the workplace, start by reading this book!"

—Daniel L. Shapiro, PhD, Author of *Negotiating the Nonnegotiable*

Peaceful Living

Daily Meditations for Living With Love,
Healing, and Compassion

By Mary Mackenzie

$19.95 — Trade Paper 5x7.5, 448pp
ISBN: 978-1-892005-19-9

Live More Authentically and Peacefully Than You Ever Dreamed Possible

In this gathering of wisdom, Mary Mackenzie empowers you with an intimate life map that will literally change the course of your life for the better. Each of the 366 meditations includes an inspirational quote and concrete, practical tips for integrating the daily message into your life. The learned behaviors of cynicism, resentment, and getting even are replaced with the skills of Nonviolent Communication, including recognizing one's needs and values and making choices in alignment with them.

Peaceful Living goes beyond daily affirmations, providing the skills and consciousness you need to transform relationships, heal pain, and discover the life-enriching meaning behind even the most trying situations. Begin each day centered and connected to yourself and your values. Direct the course of your life toward your deepest hopes and needs. Ground yourself in the power of compassionate, conscious living.

SAVE an extra 10% at NonviolentCommunication.com with code: **bookads**

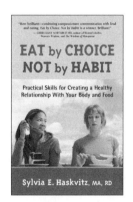

Eat by Choice, Not by Habit

Practical Skills for Creating a Healthy
Relationship With Your Body and Food

By Sylvia Haskvitz, MA, RD

$8.95 — 5-3/8x8-3/8, 128pp
ISBN: 978-1-892005-20-5

Develop a Healthy Relationship With Food!

Eating is a basic human need. But what if you are caught up in the cycles of overconsumption or emotional eating?

Using the consciousness of Nonviolent Communication, *Eat by Choice* helps you dig deeper into the emotional consciousness that underlies your eating patterns. Much more than a prescriptive fad diet, you'll learn practical strategies to develop a healthier relationship with food. Learn to enjoy the tastes, smells, and sensations of healthful eating once again.

"Face Your Stuff, or Stuff Your Face"
—anonymous

Available from PuddleDancer Press, the Center for Nonviolent Communication, all major bookstores, and Amazon.com. Distributed by Independent Publisher's Group: 800-888-4741.

271

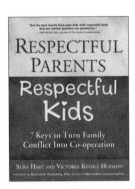

Respectful Parents, Respectful Kids

7 Keys to Turn Family Conflict Into Co-operation

By Sura Hart and Victoria Kindle Hodson

$17.95 — Trade Paper 7.5x9.25, 256pp
ISBN: 978-1-892005-22-9

Stop the Struggle—Find the Co-operation and Mutual Respect You Want!

Do more than simply correct bad behavior—finally unlock your parenting potential. Use this handbook to move beyond typical discipline techniques and begin creating an environment based on mutual respect, emotional safety, and positive, open communication. *Respectful Parents, Respectful Kids* offers *7 Simple Keys* to discover the mutual respect and nurturing relationships you've been looking for.

Use these 7 Keys to:

- Set firm limits without using demands or coercion
- Achieve mutual respect without being submissive
- Successfully prevent, reduce, and resolve conflicts
- Empower your kids to open up, co-operate, and realize their full potential
- Make your home a *No-Fault Zone* where trust thrives

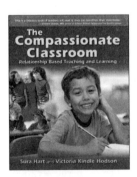

The Compassionate Classroom

Relationship Based Teaching and Learning

By Sura Hart and Victoria Kindle Hodson

$17.95 — Trade Paper 7.5x9.25, 208pp
ISBN: 978-1-892005-06-9

When Compassion Thrives, So Does Learning!

Learn powerful skills to create an emotionally safe learning environment where academic excellence thrives. Build trust, reduce conflict, improve co-operation, and maximize the potential of each student as you create relationship-centered classrooms. This how-to guide offers customizable exercises, activities, charts, and cutouts that make it easy for educators to create lesson plans for a day, a week, or an entire school year. An exceptional resource for educators, homeschool parents, child-care providers, and mentors.

"Education is not simply about teachers covering a curriculum; it is a dance of relationships. *The Compassionate Classroom* presents both the case for teaching compassionately and a wide range of practical tools to maximize student potential."

—Tim Seldin, president, The Montessori Foundation

Available from PuddleDancer Press, the Center for Nonviolent Communication, all major bookstores, and Amazon.com. Distributed by Independent Publisher's Group: 800-888-4741.

272

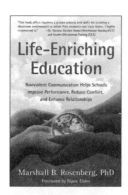

Life-Enriching Education

Nonviolent Communication Helps Schools Improve Performance, Reduce Conflict, and Enhance Relationships

By Marshall B. Rosenberg, PhD

$15.95 — Trade Paper 6x9, 192pp
ISBN: 978-1-892005-05-2

Maximize Every Student's Potential!

Filled with insight, adaptable exercises, and role-plays, *Life-Enriching Education* gives educators practical skills to generate mutually respectful classroom relationships. Discover how our language and organizational structures directly impact student potential, trust, self-esteem, and student enjoyment in their learning. Rediscover the joy of teaching in a classroom where each person's needs are respected!

NVC Will Empower You to:
- Get to the heart of classroom conflicts quickly
- Listen so students are really heard
- Maximize the individual potential of all students
- Strengthen student interest, retention, and connection to their schoolwork
- Improve trust and connection in your classroom community
- Let go of unhealthy, coercive teaching styles
- Improve classroom teamwork, efficiency, and co-operation

SAVE an extra 10% at NonviolentCommunication.com with code: **bookads**

The No-Fault Classroom

Tools to Resolve Conflict & Foster Relationship Intelligence

By Sura Hart and Victoria Kindle Hodson

$17.95 — Trade Paper 8.5x11, 256pp
ISBN: 978-1-892005-18-2

Students Can Resolve Their Own Conflicts!

Offering far more than discipline techniques that move aggressive behavior out of the classroom to the playground or sidewalk, *The No-Fault Classroom* leads students ages 7–12 to develop skills in problem solving, empathic listening, and conflict resolution that will last a lifetime.

The book's twenty-one interactive and step-by-step lessons, construction materials, and adaptable scripts give educators the tools they need to return order and co-operation to the classroom and jumpstart engaged learning—from the rural school to the inner city, the charter school, to the home school classroom. *Curricular Tie-ins* guide teachers to use the conflict resolution tools they've developed to meet state learning requirements in social studies, language arts, history, reading, and science.

Available from PuddleDancer Press, the Center for Nonviolent Communication, all major bookstores, and Amazon.com. Distributed by Independent Publisher's Group: 800-888-4741.

Being Me, Loving You: *A Practical Guide to Extraordinary Relationships* **by Marshall B. Rosenberg, PhD** • Watch your relationships strengthen as you learn to think of love as something you "do," something you give freely from the heart.
80pp, ISBN: 978-1-892005-16-8 • **$6.95**

Getting Past the Pain Between Us: *Healing and Reconciliation Without Compromise* **by Marshall B. Rosenberg, PhD** • Learn simple steps to create the heartfelt presence necessary for lasting healing to occur—great for mediators, counselors, families, and couples.
48pp, ISBN: 978-1-892005-07-6 • **$6.95**

Graduating From Guilt: *Six Steps to Overcome Guilt and Reclaim Your Life* **by Holly Michelle Eckert** • The burden of guilt leaves us stuck, stressed, and feeling like we can never measure up. Through a proven six-step process, this book helps liberate you from the toxic guilt, blame, and shame you carry.
96pp, ISBN: 978-1-892005-23-6 • **$7.95**

The Heart of Social Change: *How to Make a Difference in Your World* **by Marshall B. Rosenberg, PhD** • Learn how creating an internal consciousness of compassion can impact your social change efforts.
48pp, ISBN: 978-1-892005-10-6 • **$6.95**

Humanizing Health Care: *Creating Cultures of Compassion With Nonviolent Communication* **by Melanie Sears, RN, MBA, PhD** • Leveraging more than twenty-five years nursing experience, Melanie demonstrates the profound effectiveness of NVC to create lasting, positive improvements to patient care and the health care workplace.
112pp, ISBN: 978-1-892005-26-7 • **$7.95**

Parenting From Your Heart: *Sharing the Gifts of Compassion, Connection, and Choice* **by Inbal Kashtan** • Filled with insight and practical skills, this booklet will help you transform your parenting to address every day challenges.
48pp, ISBN: 978-1-892005-08-3 • **$6.95**

Practical Spirituality: *Reflections on the Spiritual Basis of Nonviolent Communication* **by Marshall B. Rosenberg, PhD** • Marshall's views on the spiritual origins and underpinnings of NVC, and how practicing the process helps him connect to the Divine.
48pp, ISBN: 978-1-892005-14-4 • **$6.95**

Raising Children Compassionately: *Parenting the Nonviolent Communication Way* **by Marshall B. Rosenberg, PhD** • Learn to create a mutually respectful, enriching family dynamic filled with heartfelt communication.
32pp, ISBN: 978-1-892005-09-0 • **$5.95**

The Surprising Purpose of Anger: *Beyond Anger Management: Finding the Gift* **by Marshall B. Rosenberg, PhD** • Marshall shows you how to use anger to discover what you need, and then how to meet your needs in more constructive, healthy ways.
48pp, ISBN: 978-1-892005-15-1 • **$6.95**

Teaching Children Compassionately: *How Students and Teachers Can Succeed With Mutual Understanding* **by Marshall B. Rosenberg, PhD** • In this national keynote address to Montessori educators, Marshall describes his progressive, radical approach to teaching that centers on compassionate connection.
48pp, ISBN: 978-1-892005-11-3 • **$6.95**

We Can Work It Out: *Resolving Conflicts Peacefully and Powerfully* **by Marshall B. Rosenberg, PhD** • Practical suggestions for fostering empathic connection, genuine co-operation, and satisfying resolutions in even the most difficult situations.
32pp, ISBN: 978-1-892005-12-0 • **$5.95**

What's Making You Angry? *10 Steps to Transforming Anger So Everyone Wins* **by Shari Klein and Neill Gibson** • A powerful, step-by-step approach to transform anger to find healthy, mutually satisfying outcomes.
32pp, ISBN: 978-1-892005-13-7 • **$5.95**

Available from PuddleDancer Press, the Center for Nonviolent Communication, all major bookstores, and Amazon.com. Distributed by IPG: 800-888-4741. For more information about these booklets or to order online, visit www.NonviolentCommunication.com

About the Editor

Mary Goyer, MS, is a holistic counselor and trainer who specializes in leadership and personal development at work and at home. In her practice, she draws upon her traditional training in marriage and family therapy, her background in Nonviolent Communication, and her expertise in mind-body healing techniques to help professionals in struggling teams tap into their creative, collaborative potential.

Mary spent the first part of her career as an educator, counselor, and consultant working with at-risk tweens and teens. After years of supporting students directly, she now focuses on providing professional development for educators. Mary's passion for cultivating community through interpersonal skills trainings is part of her holistic approach to support sustainability and resiliency among educators and ultimately help students grow into contributing, balanced adults. This passion has inspired numerous corporate and school partnership projects that aim to provide schools with social-emotional programming resources for students, teachers, and parents.

Meanwhile, Mary continues to bring her warm, interdisciplinary approach to her work with busy professionals. In private practice, she combines her training, coaching, and counseling backgrounds to help leaders cultivate the collaboration skills that make a true impact—at work, at home, and in the larger community.

See more at www.consciouscommunication.co.